GW01458580

A Musical Play

by

DAVID WOOD

SAMUEL FRENCH

LONDON

NEW YORK SYDNEY TORONTO HOLLYWOOD

ISBN 0 573 05033 3

Printed in Great Britain by W & J Mackay Limited, Chatham

FLIBBERTY AND THE PENGUIN was first presented by the WORCES-
TER REPERTORY COMPANY on Boxing Day, 1971, at the Swan
Theatre, Worcester, with the following cast of characters:

The Penguin	*Penny Jones*
Flibberty Gibbet	*John A. Cooper*
a friendly goblin	
The Three-Headed Knowall	*Peter Wickham*
	John Bleasdale
	Anna Nicholas
Krafty Kingfisher	*Frank Ellis*
Mr Silly Cuckoo	*Leslie Glazer*
Mrs Silly Cuckoo	*Jenny Burke*
The Bus Driver/Conductor	*Roger Milner*
Mr Maestro	*Don Dryden*
a famous conductor	
Master Ministrone	*Harvey Edwards*
his assistant	
The Policeman	*John Rainer*
The Zookeeper	*Peter Wickham*
Father Penguin	*John Bleasdale*
Mother Penguin	*Anna Nicholas*

The play directed by **John Hole**

Choreography by **Judy Stephens**

Designed by **Louanne Harvey**

The action takes place in a clearing in the Forest, at the River Bank, in
another part of the Forest, at the Bus Stop, in the Town, inside the Police
Station, at the Zoo, and in the Concert Hall.

AUTHOR'S NOTE

It could be argued that a production of a play for children demands three virtues—pace, clarity and sincerity.

Pace, not to be confused with sheer speed, is necessary to ensure the audience's continued excitement and interest. Simplicity of production often helps this—too much time spent on scene changes in black-outs may well sabotage the atmosphere and exposition of the previous scene, and also stifle the imagination of the children who may well enjoy the mime necessitated by a stylized set more than the obvious employment of a totally realistic one.

Clarity is obviously essential to establish character and plot: if the audience fails to understand what is happening their interest will soon dwindle.

Sincerity will ensure involvement and belief. There should be no "playing to the adults" or patronizing. The story, played for real, will help to achieve an excited and exciting response.

NOTE ON THE CHARACTERS: The Three-Headed Knowall can be doubled by the Zookeeper, Father Penguin and Mother Penguin. The plot is partly dependent upon the fact that Mr Maestro, in full evening dress—tails, etc.—looks very similar to the Penguins. Similarly Master Ministrone and Flibberty Gibbet, though not dressed the same, are physically alike. The Penguin and his parents never speak. Mr Maestro never speaks, only sings.

SONGS

ACT I

1. "The Penguin"	**Flibberty and Audience**
2. "Three Heads are Better than One"	**Three-Headed Knowall**
3. "My Kingdom for a Fish!"	**Krafty Kingfisher, Flibberty**
4. "Oo-cuck!"	**Mr and Mrs Silly Cuckoo**
5. "Come for a ride"	**The Bus Conductor and Three-Headed Knowall**
6. "Come for a ride" (Reprise)	**The Bus Conductor and Mr and Mrs Silly Cuckoo**
7. "Peck that Penguin"	**Krafty Kingfisher**
8. "Music is Magic"	**Mr Maestro, Master Ministrone, Policeman**
9. "What a Bella Bella Bell!"	**Mr Maestro, Master Ministrone, Bus Conductor**

ACT II

1. "Count up to ten"	**Policeman and Company and Audience**
2. "In the Zoo"	**Bus Conductor, Flibberty**
3. "In the Zoo" (Reprise)	**Bus Conductor, Flibberty**
4. "Roll up! Roll up!"	**Zookeeper**
5. "Roll up! Roll up!" (Reprise)	**Zookeeper**
6. "The First Day of Spring"	**Company and Audience**
7. "Goodbye, Penguins" and "Come for a Ride" (Reprise)	**Company**

ACT I

SCENE 1

A forest clearing. Late wintertime

Music is heard as the Penguin enters upstage, carrying a small suitcase. He is clearly tired after a long journey and, seeing a convenient log under a tree, he decides to have a rest and sits down. As he dozes off an acorn drops from the tree and wakes him up. He closes his eyes again, but another acorn falls. This time he looks up, sees nothing, and tries to sleep again. Another acorn falls on his head, followed by another, and another, until a stream of acorns pours down from the tree, accompanied by gleeful laughter. Mystified, the Penguin runs out of the firing-line and looks up into the branches. Suddenly he sees a laughing face come through the leaves. It is Flibberty Gibbet, a goblin

Flibberty Hallo!

The Penguin does not answer, but sadly rubs the top of his head

I didn't hurt you, did I? They're only acorns.

The Penguin nods as Flibberty jumps down from the tree and comes up to him

I'm sorry. Look, I'm Flibberty.

The Penguin puts his head on one side enquiringly

Flibberty. Well, Flibberty Gibbet, really, but that's too long for anyone to remember, so everyone calls me Flibberty. I'm a goblin. What are you?

The Penguin points to himself, but makes no reply

Yes, but what *are* you?

The Penguin shrugs his shoulders, points to his beak, and shakes his head

What's the matter? Can't you speak?

The Penguin shakes his head

Oh dear! You poor thing. That must make life very difficult for you. I mean, I don't even know what you are. I've never seen anything like . . . (*Noticing the audience, he speaks to them*) *You* don't know what he is, do you?

Audience participation

A what? A Penguin? (*To the Penguin*) Is that right?

The Penguin nods

Where have you come from?

The Penguin mimes being very cold, shuddering, slapping himself to keep warm. From now on the audience is encouraged to interpret the Penguin's mimes. Flibberty appears to be somewhat slower than the audience, so that half their fun is guessing what the Penguin is "saying" before Flibberty can guess. Flibberty will have to improvise somewhat, but as long as the sequence of mimes is always the same there should be no problem

(*To the Audience*) What's he saying? He looks cold, doesn't he? Where? Iceland? (*To the Penguin*) Is that right?

The Penguin nods

(*To the audience*) Oh, well done! (*To the Penguin*) How did you get from Iceland all the way here?

The Penguin mimes "walking". The audience shout this out

You walked?

The Penguin nods, then mimes "swimming"

And swam across the sea?

The Penguin nods, then mimes "climbing mountains"

And climbed mountains? My, no wonder you look tired. But why have you come here, to this forest?

The Penguin mimes "searching for someone"

Looking for someone?

The Penguin mimes "not one person, two people"

Two people. (*To the audience*) Who could they be?

The Penguin opens his case and takes out a framed photo of his father and mother

Who are they? (*Helped by the audience*) Your mother and father?

The Penguin nods

Well, where are they?

The Penguin shrugs his shoulders

Where? Oh, you don't know. Of course, that's why you're looking for them. What happened to them?

The Penguin mimes "I don't know, they just disappeared"

What? They disappeared?

The Penguin nods and begins to sob

And you've come all this way to find them?

The Penguin nods, sobbing

Oh! (*To the audience*) Well, I think we ought to help him, don't you? Shall we help him?

Hearing the audience reaction, the Penguin brightens considerably and jumps around, delighted

We'll help you find them.

The Penguin shows signs of being very hot after his leaping about

What's the matter? (*Encouraged by the audience*) You're too hot?

The Penguin nods

Well, if you're used to living in Iceland, I'm not surprised. Even in winter here, it's warmer than in Iceland. Take your coat off.

The Penguin mimes that he cannot—his "coat" is part of him

Oh I see. No wonder you're hot. Now look, we'd better get started. Spring's on the way, you know. And then the weather begins to get hotter. We *must* find your mother and father before then, otherwise you'll roast! By the way, what's your name?

The Penguin shrugs his shoulders

You don't know? (*Helped by the audience*) You haven't got one? Well, you must have a name. (*He has an idea. To the audience*) Can anyone think of a good name for a Penguin? (*He chooses one from the names shouted out by the audience*)

Every performance the Penguin could have a different name. For the sake of clarity in the script, he will be called "Percival"

Percival! That's a good name. Do you like it, Percival?

The Penguin nods

Good.

SONG: THE PENGUIN SONG

> (*Singing*) He's Percival
> The Penguin
> He's Percival
> The Penguin
> From the land of ice and snow.
> He's Percival
> The Penguin
> And I think he's very nice to know.

(*After one verse*) Look, I tell you what. *You* chose the name for Percival, so whenever the word "Percival" comes up in the song, I'll wave—and would you like to sing "Percival" as loud as you flibberty well can? Then Percival will realize how many friends he's got.

Flibberty continues to sing, the audience joining in with the name

He's Percival
The Penguin
He's Percival
The Penguin
From the land of ice and snow.
He's Percival
The Penguin
And I think he's very nice to know.

He's white on his middle
And black on his back
There's a waddle in his walk
It's rather a riddle
He can't even quack
Or chirp or cheep or talk.

He's Percival
The Penguin
He's Percival
The Penguin
Searching for his mum and dad.
He's Percival
The Penguin
If we find them then he won't be sad.

Some tasty smoked kippers
He fancies to eat
Opens wide his orange beak
He flaps with his flippers
He taps his webbed feet
For Penguins cannot speak.

He's Percival
The Penguin
He's Percival
The Penguin
From the land of ice and snow.
He's Percival
The Penguin
And I think he's very nice to know.

During the song the Penguin dances happily

Come on, Percival, let's start looking for your mother and **father**— (*remembering the photo*)—don't forget your photo and the case.

The Penguin goes to pick up the case

What else have you brought with you?

The Penguin brings out a toothbrush

What's that? (*Helped by the audience*) A toothbrush?

The Penguin nods and brings out a large bar of soap

And a bar of soap?

The Penguin nods

Is that all?

The Penguin nods

Well, let's hope they come in useful. Come on, let's go and find the Three-Headed Knowall.

The Penguin nods. They set off. The Penguin stops and looks as if to say "who?"

Who? The Three-Headed Knowall—if anyone in the forest knows where your mother and father are, *he* will, because he's three times as brainy as anyone else.

The Penguin looks up enquiringly

Why? Because he's got three heads, that's why! Come on.

Flibberty drags the bewildered Penguin off.

The Three-Headed Knowall enters from the opposite side. He is a stately, pompous creature, whose three heads all look similar and can speak individually or simultaneously. Head Three is not as brainy as Heads One and Two, but tries very hard. Heads One and Two are conscious of their superiority

SONG: THREE HEADS ARE BETTER THAN ONE

All Heads (*singing*)

Three heads are better than one
Three heads are better than two
The Three-Headed Knowall
Knows all there is to know
When, where, what, why, which, who?

For
One head is better than none
But one's not as useful as two
With three heads be certain
There's nothing I don't know
When, where, what, why, which, who?

If you can't find a sock
If you think you've lost your way
If you can't read the clock
If you can't think what to do on a
Rainy day

	If a sum looks absurd
	And you're getting in a fuss
	If you can't spell a word
Head One	Ask me
Head Two	Ask me
Head Three	Ask me
All Heads	Ask us!

Yes
Three heads are better than one
Three heads are better than two
The Three-Headed Knowall
Knows all there is to know
When, where, what, why, which, who?

Head One Two
Head Two Two's are
Head Three Four.
Head One ⎫ Good.   ⎧ *Speaking*
Head Two ⎭   ⎩ *together*
Head One Two
Head Two Three's are
Head Three (*after a moment of concentration*) Six.
Head One ⎫ Excellent.   ⎧ *Speaking*
Head Two ⎭   ⎩ *together*
Head One Two
Head Two Fours are
Head Three (*hesitating*) Eight?
Head One ⎫ Brilliant.   ⎧ *Speaking*
Head Two ⎭   ⎩ *together*
Head One Two
Head Two Fives are
Head Three (*after an agonizing pause*) Thirteen?
Head One ⎫ (*viciously turning on Head Three*) No, no,   ⎧ *Speaking*
Head Two ⎭ wrong again. Two fives are *ten. TEN.*   ⎩ *together*
Head Three I'm sorry, Head One. I'm sorry, Head Two.
Head One ⎫ What is the use of being a Three-Headed   ⎧ *Speaking*
Head Two ⎭ Knowall if one head knows less than the   ⎩ *together*
              other two. Now, poetry time.
Head Three I'll get this right, Heads One and Two, I promise.
Head One Little
Head Two Jack
Head Three Horner
Head One Sat
Head Two In the
Head Three (*looking pleased*) Corner
Head One Eating
Head Two His
Head Three Curds and whey.

Head One (*looking concerned*) He put in
Head Two (*looking concerned*) His
Head Three Thumb

Heads One and Two look relieved

Head One And pulled
Head Two Out a
Head Three Spider
Head One (*looking angry*) And
Head Two (*looking angry*) Said
Head Three (*trying very hard*) This little piggy eats roast beef!
Head One } No, no, wrong again!   { *Speaking*
Head Two }   { *together*

Flibberty and the Penguin enter

Wrong again! (*Seeing Flibberty and the Penguin*) Sssh! Visitors. Now don't let us down.
Head Three I'll do my best.
Head One } Sssh!   { *Speaking*
Head Two }   { *together*

Flibberty goes up to the Three-Headed Knowall

Flibberty Hello, hello, hello, Three-Headed Knowall. Good morning, good morning, good morning.
All Heads Good day, Flibberty.
Flibberty How are you, how are you, how are you?
All Heads There's no need to be flippant, Flibberty. Just say it once. That's quite sufficient.
Flibberty All right, all right, all right.
Head One (*menacing*) I
Head Two (*menacing*) Beg
Head Three (*menacing*) Your
All Heads (*menacing*) Pardon?
Flibberty (*taken aback*) All right.
All Heads That's better.
Head One (*looking at the Penguin*) Tell me
Head Two (*looking at the Penguin*) Who
Head Three (*looking at the Penguin*) Is
All Heads (*looking at the Penguin*) That?

The Penguin trembles, frightened

Flibberty That, Three-Headed Knowall, is my friend Percival the Penguin.
All Heads Ahhhhhh!
Head One (*to Head Two*) A Penguin!
Head Two (*to Head One*) A Penguin!
Head Three A Penguin? (*To Heads One and Two*) What is a Penguin?
Head One } Sssh! (*In a loud whisper to Head Three*)   { *Speaking*
Head Two } The Three-Headed Knowall is expected to   { *together*
           know all. Don't make me look stupid.

Head Three I'm sorry.
Head One (*to Flibberty*) What can I do
Head Two For your friend
Head Three The—er—pencil?
Head One ⎫ *No, the Penguin.*   ⎰ *Speaking*
Head Two ⎭   ⎱ *together*
All Heads What can we do for him?
Flibberty He's lost his mother and father.
Head One Oh
Head Two Poor
Head Three Er—Peppermint.
Head One ⎫ *No. Penguin!*   ⎰ *Speaking*
Head Two ⎭   ⎱ *together*
All Heads How can we help?
Flibberty Tell us where we might find them.
Head One Oh, but recently we
Head Two Haven't seen any
Head Three Er—pincushions.
Head One ⎫ *No—Penguins!*   ⎰ *Speaking*
Head Two ⎭   ⎱ *together*
Flibberty But where would be a good place to look?
All Heads Let me think.

All three Heads adopt thinking poses

Head One (*suddenly*) Why
Head Two Not try
Head Three The town?
Head One ⎱ *No—(realizing)—yes.* (*To Head Three*) Good ⎰ *Speaking*
Head Two ⎰ idea, Head Three.   ⎱ *together*

Head Three smiles

All Heads Why not try the town?
Flibberty The town? I've never been there before. Who should I ask there?
All Heads Let me think.

The Heads adopt more thinking poses. Suddenly they all go to utter, but think better of it and return to their thinking poses. This is repeated

Head One ⎫   ⎧ *suddenly* ⎫ Why don't . . .   ⎧ *Speaking*
Head Two ⎬   ⎨ *suddenly* ⎬ What about . . .   ⎨
Head Three ⎭ ⎩ *suddenly* ⎭ How about . . .   ⎩ *together*
Head One (*to Head Two, very politely*) So sorry.
Head Two (*to Head Three, very politely*) After you.
Head Three (*to Head One*) I beg your pardon.
Head One (*to Head Three*) Not at all.
Head Two (*to Head One*) Do go on.
Head Three (*to Head Two*) Thank you—why not ask a policeman?
Flibberty A policeman?

Head One⎤ Of course. A policeman. (*To Head* ⎧*Speaking*
Head Two ⎦ *Three*) Well done, Head Three. ⎩*together*
Head Three Thank you, Head One. Thank you, Head Two.

The three Heads beam with pleasure

Flibberty Thank you, Three-Headed Knowall. Come on, Percival, let's go to town and find a policeman.

Flibberty and the Penguin start to move

Wait a minute. Where *is* the town? Can you tell us, Three-Headed Know-all?
All Heads Of course. Easy. The town is in *that* direction.

Head One and Two point one way and Head Three points another

Flibberty (*confused*) Where?
All Heads There!

Head Two suddenly realizes that Head Three is pointing in a different direction

Head Two (*calling*) Head One!
Head One Yes, Head Two?
Head Two Look at Head Three.

Head One does so

Head One ⎤
Head Two ⎦ Oh dear. Head Three! Get it right! ⎧*Speaking*
⎩*together*
Head Three (*realizing*) Oh, I'm so sorry, I was certain it was in *that* direction . . .
Head One ⎤ What is the use of a Three-Headed Knowall ⎧*Speaking*
Head Two ⎦ if one head is stupid, stupid, stupid?, etc. ⎩*together*
Head Three Please give me another chance, etc.

The Three-Headed Knowall exits, arguing with itself

Flibberty (*calling after it*) But which way is the town? (*But the Three-Headed Knowall has gone*) Oh dear. We're still none the flibberty wiser.

The Penguin pats his stomach and looks uncomfortable

What's the matter? (*Helped by the audience*) Are you hungry?

The Penguin nods

Haven't you eaten since you left Iceland?

The Penguin shakes his head

Well, let's think. What would you like? (*Half thinking, half to the audience*) What do penguins like to eat? (*Hearing "fish" from the audience*) Fish? (*To the Penguin*) Do you like fish?

The Penguin nods and looks excited by the idea

Where can we get some fish? In the river, I suppose. *I* know—we'll ask Krafty Kingfisher—he fishes every day, over on the other bank. We'll have to go over the stepping-stones. Be careful, Percival, they're very slippery. Come on.

MIME SEQUENCE TO MUSIC

Flibberty and the Penguin set off for the river bank; they walk round the stage until Flibberty indicates the river. Gingerly they step on the "stepping stones". There is fun as the Penguin nearly falls in the river and is just saved by Flibberty. At one point the Penguin has one foot on one stone and one on another, and gets stuck. Flibberty has to go back a few stones to lift the Penguin's back foot off and put it on the next stone. But the Penguin nearly loses his balance and as the nimble Flibberty leaps over the next stone, the Penguin saves himself by putting his back foot on the last stone. This is repeated. Eventually they arrive at the other side of the river, where we suddenly see Krafty Kingfisher sitting with his fishing-rod and wicker basket. He is in a bad mood because, as we later discover, he has caught nothing. The music ends as Flibberty and the Penguin "set foot on dry land"! The Penguin is still shaking from the ordeal

(*Whispering*) All right?

The Penguin nods bravely

Now, there he is. Krafty Kingfisher. Whatever you do, don't be rude to him. He can be very bad-tempered. And, when cross, he can paralyse you with a very painful poisonous peck with his beak!

The Penguin looks worried

Don't worry. Come on.

Flibberty and the Penguin move towards Krafty Kingfisher. As they near him he pulls in his fishing line

Excuse us.

Kingfisher (*furious at finding nothing on the hook*) Ahhh! Bejubejubejubejub.

Flibberty and the Penguin run away in fright

Nothing. Nothing.

Flibberty and the Penguin gingerly approach again as Krafty Kingfisher casts off and pulls in the line again

Flibberty Krafty Kingfisher . . .

Kingfisher (*finding nothing on his hook as before*) Ahhhh! Bejubejubejubejub. Nothing, nothing.

Flibberty and the Penguin run away again in fright. Krafty Kingfisher casts off once more, and pulls in the line as Flibberty and the Penguin approach one last time

Flibberty Excuse me, Krafty Kingfisher . . .

This time there is something pulling on the line—Krafty Kingfisher is very excited—too excited to be angered by the interruption

Kingfisher What is it, what is it? Oh! Jubbyjubbyjubby! (*Struggling with his rod*) Can't you see I'm busy?

Flibberty I'm sorry, but . . .

Kingfisher (*forced to stand up by the pressure on his rod*) Well, don't just stand there—help me! It must be a *huge* pike or perch at least.

Flibberty hangs on to the rod. The Penguin hovers behind

Right. Easy does it. Easy does it. Oh! Jubbyjubbyjub! Here it comes. (*Slowly he pulls the line up, to reveal a large old boot on the hook*) Ahhhh! Bejubejubejubejub!

Flibberty laughs and tries to restrain himself

A boot! I can't eat a boot! (*Seeing Flibberty*) What's the matter with you? (*He advances menacingly on Flibberty*)

Flibberty Nothing, Krafty Kingfisher.

Kingfisher Do you want me to give you a painful, poisonous peck?

Flibberty N—n—no.

Kingfisher (*seeing the Penguin*) Who are you?

The Penguin trembles and flaps his arms about

Speak up. Speak up. Lost your voice? Do you want a painful, poisonous peck to bring it back?

Flibberty (*intervening*) He can't speak, Krafty Kingfisher. He's my friend Percival the Penguin, all the way from Iceland. He's very hungry.

Kingfisher That makes two of us. I'm starving.

Flibberty But what about the fish? Percival was hoping you could spare him some.

Kingfisher Huh! Certainly not. I can't catch any for myself, let alone him.

Flibberty But why can't you catch any?

Kingfisher It's winter, isn't it? It's cold. No fish with any sense would hang around here. They've swum somewhere warmer. Only a few stupid fish left—and I've caught most of them already. Now clear off, I can't sit around talking to you.

Flibberty But . . .

Kingfisher Clear off!

The vehemence of this sends Flibberty and the Penguin off to the other side of the stage

MUSIC starts for song

Flibberty We'd better try and find the town, Percival.

The Penguin mimes that he's tired

Are you tired? Well, let's sit down and rest for a while.

Flibberty and the Penguin sit down in such a position that when Krafty

Kingfisher catches something and swings it back over his head, it falls into their laps. The Penguin dozes off, while Flibberty keeps watch

SONG : MY KINGDOM FOR A FISH

Kingfisher (*singing*)
Each day I squat here in the cold
Waiting patiently.
I squat here with my rod
Thinking of my tea.
I imagine a fish, see it frying on the fire—
Feel a bite—pull it in—and it's a bicycle tyre.

Krafty Kingfisher pulls in a bicycle tyre. It swings over to Flibberty, who is surprised and then disappointed

A fish, a fish
My kingdom for a fish
Not rubbish or junk or slime.
I wish, I wish
For a fish for my dish
Oh where do fishes go in wintertime.

Krafty Kingfisher prepares to cast off again

With bated breath and baited hook
Staring at the stream
I crave a juicy carp
Or a tasty bream
And I savour its smell, hear it sizzle in the pan
Feel a bite—pull it in—and it's an old tin can.

Krafty Kingfisher pulls in a tin can, which swings over to Flibberty as before

A fish, a fish
The Penguin needs a fish
Not rubbish or junk or slime.
I wish, I wish
For a fish for his dish

Flibberty   ⎫
Kingfisher ⎬ Oh where do fishes go in wintertime. ⎰ *Singing*
                                                      ⎱ *together*
Kingfisher   With feathers frozen, beak turned blue
Sitting shivering
For hours my line is still
Hardly quivering.
Must I starve? Just one catch—that's
My dream, that is my wish!
Feel a bite—pull it in—it can't be—
It's a fish!

Krafty Kingfisher pulls in a fish and swings it over to Flibberty

	A fish, a fish	
	It is, it is a fish	
Flibberty	Not rubbish or junk or slime	*Singing*
Kingfisher	A fish, a fish,	*together*
	A fish for his/my dish	
	Tonight he's/I'm gonna have a jubby time.	

Kingfisher Jubby Jubby Jubby Jubby Jub. At last.

Flibberty Hey! Percival! (*He wakes up the Penguin*) A fish! (*He quickly takes the fish off the hook*) Quick—run! (*To the audience*) Don't tell him it was us, *please.*

Flibberty and the Penguin run off

Krafty Kingfisher greedily swings the line back

Kingfisher A fish! A fish! Jubby Jubby Jubby. (*He sees the end of the line—empty*) Aaahh, bejubejubejubejub. It's gone! (*He looks off, and clearly catches a glimpse of Flibberty*) Flibberty!! (*To the audience, very angrily*) Did Flibberty pinch my fish? (*The audience should say "No"*) Did he? ("*No*") Oh yes, he did. He pinched it for that Penguin, didn't he? ("*No*") Oh yes, he did. ("*Oh no, he didn't*") Right—Penguin, you've had it now. I'll give him a painful poisonous peck. (*He starts to move off*) Just you wait! (*He stops*) And—(*to the audience*)—don't you tell lies to me again— or I'll give *you all* a painful poisonous peck. Aaahh Bejubejubejubejub.

Krafty Kingfisher exits savagely.

SCENE 2

Another part of the forest

Mrs Silly Cuckoo, bossy and irritable, enters calling

Mrs Silly Cuckoo Mr Silly Cuckoo! Mr Silly Cuckoo!! "Urry 'urry up!"

Mr Silly Cuckoo enters breathlessly, with a shopping bag

Mr Silly Cuckoo Mrs Silly Cuckoo, I'm 'urry 'urrying as fast as my leggy pegs will go.

Mrs Silly Cuckoo At lasty-wasty! Where on earthy-wearthy have you beeny-weeny?

Mr Silly Cuckoo I'm sorry, Mrs Silly Cuckoo. But I've got all your shoppy-wopping to carry-warry.

Mrs Silly Cuckoo Then put it downy-wowny for a seccy-weccy, Mr Silly Cuckoo. Oh, you're such a silly-willy-billy. Wool! (*She hands him a ball of wool and starts knitting*)

Mr Silly Cuckoo I'm sorry-worry, Mrs Silly Cuckoo. (*He puts down the shopping*) I'm a teeny weeny bit hot and bother-wothered today.

Mrs Silly Cuckoo Ah! That's because it will soon be the first day of springy-wingy.

Mr Silly Cuckoo Of course. How luviwuviduvly! The first day of springy-wingy.

They giggle

Mrs Silly Cuckoo Warmer weather round the corner-worner.

Mr Silly Cuckoo How excitiwiting. Soon I'll be the first cuckoo of springy-wingy. Everyone will hear me singalinging my song and know that springywingy's here. Ah!

Mrs Silly Cuckoo (*after a stunned pause*) I beg your pardon?

Mr Silly Cuckoo (*delighted*) I shall be the first cuckoo of springywingy.

Mrs Silly Cuckoo (*furiously*) Oh no you willy notwot.

Mr Silly Cuckoo But, Mrs Silly Cuckoo . . .

Mrs Silly Cuckoo *I* shallywall.

Mr Silly Cuckoo But you were firstywirsty *last* year!

Mrs Silly Cuckoo Exactlywactly. I was *so* goodygood last year that I shall be firstywirsty again *this* year.

Mr Silly Cuckoo But that's not fair. It's my turnywurn. Any anyway, last year you sang your cuckoos so badly that no-one heard them till the *fourth* day of springywingy.

Mrs Silly Cuckoo You cheeky-beaky bird! I'd like to hear you do better-wetter.

Mr Silly Cuckoo Very well—listen. (*He clears his throat and then, in a rather cracked voice, sings "Cuckoo, cuckoo, cuckoo", but reverses the musical notes*) How's thatywat?

Mrs Silly Cuckoo Terriwerrible! You go up instead of down an down instead of up. It's "la la", not "la la". (*She "La's" the correct cuckoo notes*)

Mr Silly Cuckoo Well, you show me then, if you're so cleverdever.

Mrs Silly Cuckoo Very Well. (*She clears her throat and then, getting the notes right, reverses the word*) Oo-cuck, Oo-cuck, Oo-cuck. How's thatywat?

Mr Silly Cuckoo (*speaking*) Oo-cuck, oo-cuck? Oh, Mrs Silly Cuckoo, that's terriwerrible! It's *cuck-oo,* not oo-cuck.

Mrs Silly Cuckoo Well, it's better than yours, anyway. Let's try againywen, till we get it right.

SONG: OO-CUCK!

Both (*singing together*)
    We're two silly-billy cuckoos
    We don't know our cucks from our oos
    If we can't sing properwoperly
    When winter turns to spring
    How will you hear the luviduvly news?

Mrs Silly Cuckoo Oo cuck
Mr Silly Cuckoo Cuckoo
Both Will we never get it rightywight?
Mrs Silly Cuckoo Oo cuck
Mr Silly Cuckoo Cuckoo

Both	Pracywactising all nightywight
Mrs Silly Cuckoo	Oo cuck
Mr Silly Cuckoo	Cuckoo
Both	It's wrong againywen I fear
	And the first day of springywing
	Will soon be here
	We're two sillybilly cuckoos
	We can't sing our cuckoo song
Mr Silly Cuckoo	I go up instead of downywown
Mrs Silly Cuckoo	I oo when I should cuck
Both	And we've not gotiwoty very long.
Mrs Silly Cuckoo	Oo cuck
Mr Silly Cuckoo	Cuckoo
Both	Will we never get it rightywight?
Mrs Silly Cuckoo	Oo cuck
Mr Silly Cuckoo	Cuckoo
Both	Pracywactising all nightywight
Mrs Silly Cuckoo	Oo cuck
Mr Silly Cuckoo	Cuckoo
Both	It's wrong againywen I fear
	And the first day of springywing
	Will soon be here
Mrs Silly Cuckoo	Oo cuck
Mr Silly Cuckoo	Cuckoo!

Flibberty and the Penguin enter, on their way to town, still uncertain of the right directions

Flibberty It's no good, Percival, we're lost. I'm sorry, but I've no idea how to get to town.

The Penguin sees Mr and Mrs Silly Cuckoo still practising, and tries to attract Flibberty's attention to them. Flibberty misinterprets the mime

It's no use getting into a state, I've said I'm sorry. (*Realizing*) What? (*He sees Mr and Mrs Silly Cuckoo*) what about them?

The Penguin mimes "ask them the way"

Ask them the way? Good idea! Come on.

The Penguin and Flibberty approach Mr and Mrs Silly Cuckoo

Mr Silly Cuckoo ⎱	Cuckoo, cuckoo.	⎰ *Singing*
Mrs Silly Cuckoo ⎰	Oo cuck, oo cuck.	⎱ *together*

Flibberty Excuse me.
Mr Silly Cuckoo Cuckoo, cuckoo!
Mrs Silly Cuckoo Oo cuck, oo cuck!
Flibberty (*more loudly*) Excuse me.
Mrs Silly Cuckoo Don't interrupt! Oo cuck!
Mr Silly Cuckoo We're pracywactising. Cuckoo!

Flibberty What?

Mrs Silly Cuckoo We're having a pracywactice. Oo cuck!

Mr Silly Cuckoo We both want to be the first cuckoo of springywingy. Cuckoo!

Flibberty Well, you're not very good at at it, are you?

Mrs Silly Cuckoo There you are. (*To Mr Silly Cuckoo*) I told you you were terriwerrible. Oo cuck!

Flibberty (*to Mrs Silly Cuckoo*) You're even worse!

Mrs Silly Cuckoo What? How dare you. What a rude gobly woblin! What are you doing here anyway? And who's your funny friendywendy?

Flibberty This is Percival the Penguin—he's lost his mother and father. We want to know how to get to town.

Mrs Silly Cuckoo Well, *we* won't tell you—teach you not to be rudywudy.

Mr Silly Cuckoo (*whispering*) Mrs Silly Cuckoo?

Mrs Silly Cuckoo What is it, Mr Silly Cuckoo?

Mr Silly Cuckoo beckons her away and they whisper animatedly. Flibberty and the Penguin look at each other, mystified

Goodygood idea, Mr Silly Cuckoo. You tell them.

Mr Silly Cuckoo (*pleased that his idea has met with approval*) Well, Mr Goblywoblin and Mr Pennywenguin, we *will* help you get to townywown if you will help one of us to become the first cuckoo in springywingy.

Flibberty Thank you. But I can't help. You both sing very badly. Nobody would hear either of you.

The Penguin nudges Flibberty

What is it? Have you got an idea?

The Penguin nods and mimes "if they both sang together they could make more noise"

What? Both together? Of course! He says if you learned to sing together you might sing louder.

Mrs Silly Cuckoo Yes, but who could teach us to sing togetherwether? It's very trickywicky.

Flibberty Yes, you're right.

Mrs Silly Cuckoo Oh, come along, we're wasting our time, Mr Silly Cuckoo. They can't helpywelp.

The Penguin waves his arms about in the manner of a conductor

What's your friendywend doing?

Flibberty I don't know. Percival, what does that mean?

If necessary, Flibberty asks the audience, who will shout out that the Penguin is conducting

Of course—a conductor! That's what you need. A conductor could make you sing together—*and* sing the right notes.

Mrs Silly Cuckoo A conductor? Of course! Come along, Mr Silly Cuckoo.

Mr Silly Cuckoo Where are we going?

Mrs Silly Cuckoo To find a conductorwuctor.

Mr and Mrs Silly Cuckoo pick up their bags and start to exit

Mr Silly Cuckoo But what do conductorwuctors look like?
Mrs Silly Cuckoo I don't know. We'll lookylook till we find one.
Flibberty (*calling after them*) Hey!
Mrs Silly Cuckoo What is it?
Flibberty You promised to tell us how to get to town.
Mr Silly Cuckoo Catch the bus!
Flibberty The bus?
Mrs Silly Cuckoo Of course!
Flibberty But where does the bus stop?
Mrs Silly Cuckoo Don't be so sillywilly.
Mr Silly Cuckoo ⎫
Mrs Silly Cuckoo ⎬ The bus stops at the bus stop! ⎰ *Speaking*
                                                          ⎱ *together*

Mr and Mrs Silly Cuckoo exit giggling

Flibberty But where is the bus stop . . . ? (*They have gone*) Oh dear. Come on, Percival, let's start looking.

Krafty Kingfisher enters, sees Flibberty and the Penguin and exults

Kingfisher Aha! There he is—Fish Stealer! He's going to get a painful poisonous paralysing peck. (*He sharpens his beak on a tree*)

The audience shout out a warning to Flibberty and the Penguin

Flibberty and the Penguin exit

Aahhhh! Bejubejubejub! (*To the audience*) You're all nasty, rotten, beastly, horrid and I hate you! Warn that thieving penguin off again and you'll *all* get a painful, poisonous paralysing *peck*!

Krafty Kingfisher sets off after Flibberty and the Penguin

SCENE 3

The bus stop. It is on a small earth and grass mound
The Three-Headed Knowall enters

All Heads Oh, what a boring day.
Head One Nothing to do.
Head Two No-one to talk to.
Head Three Nowhere to go.
Head One No.
Head Two No.

Head Three Yes.
Head One ⎱ No!   ⎰ *Speaking*
Head Two ⎰   ⎱ *together*

The bus comes on, driven by the Conductor/Driver

Head One Ah!
Head Two Here comes
Head Three The train.
Head One ⎱ No, the bus!   ⎰ *Speaking*
Head Two ⎰   ⎱ *together*

SONG: COME FOR A RIDE

Bus Driver (*singing*)   Come for a ride
                              In my beautiful bus
                              Travel in comfort
                              No trouble or fuss
                              Come for a treat
                              Come take a seat
                              All aboard
                              My beautiful bus
                              It's cheaper than a taxi
                              Not tiring like a hike
Bus Driver   Faster than a scooter
Three-Headed   Not draughty like a bike   *Singing*
Knowall   Less bumpy than a camel   *together*
                              More spacious than a van
                              Safer than to try to
                              Fly like Peter Pan . . .

The Bus Driver "parks" at the bus stop

Three-Headed   Come, let us ride
Knowall   In this beautiful bus
                              Travel in comfort
                              No trouble, no fuss
                              Let's have a treat
                              Let's take a seat
                              Let us board
                              This beautiful bus

                              Come for a/Let us ride
                              In my/This beautiful bus
                              Travel in comfort
Bus Driver   No trouble, no fuss.
Three-Headed   Come for a/Let's have a treat *Singing*
Knowall   Come take/Let's take a seat   *together*
                              All aboard/Let us board
                              My/This beautiful bus.

Bus Driver All aboard. All aboard for the town. Non-stop to town.

All Heads Shall I go for a ride?

Head Two (*to Head One*) What do you think, Head One?

Head One (*to Head Two*) Why not, Head Two?

Head Two Shall we bother to ask Head Three, Head One?

Head One Waste of time, Head Two. Just say we're going, and tell him to buy the ticket.

Head Two Very well. Did you hear that, Head Three?

Head Three Yes, Head Two.

Head One Do it properly.

Head Three I'll do my best, Head One.

The Three-Headed Knowall advances to the bus

Bus Driver All aboard. All aboard.

Head Three I wish to buy a ticket, please.

Bus Driver Well, don't ask me, chum, I'm the driver. You want to ask the conductor.

Head Three The conductor? Of course. Oh dear.

Head One ⎱ Get on with it, Head Three. Don't flap.　⎰ *Speaking*
Head Two ⎰　　　　　　　　　　　　　　　　　　　　⎱ *together*

Head Three Yes, Heads One and Two. Where is the conductor, please, driver?

Bus Driver Inside the bus, of course.

Head Three Of course. Thank you.

Head One ⎱ Will Head Three never learn, Head One/Two?　⎰ *Speaking*
Head Two ⎰　　　　　　　　　　　　　　　　　　　　　⎱ *together*

The Three-Headed Knowall moves from the driver's cab to the entrance

Bus Driver All aboard. All aboard. (*As he shouts he changes his hat to a conductor's hat and moves inside the bus*) Any more fares, please? Any more fares?

Head Three (*arriving at the bus*) Could I have a ticket, please?

Conductor Certainly, sir.

Head Three Oh, but haven't I seen you somewhere before?

Conductor No idea, sir.

Head Three Aren't you the driver?

Conductor Oh no, sir, I'm the conductor. (*Patronizingly*) I sell the tickets. The driver drives the bus.

Head Three But . . .

Head One ⎱ (*calling*) Head Three!　⎰ *Speaking*
Head Two ⎰　　　　　　　　　　　⎱ *together*

Head Three Yes, Heads One and Two?

Head One ⎱ You're being stupid again.　⎰ *Speaking*
Head Two ⎰　　　　　　　　　　　　　⎱ *together*

Head Three But the driver and the conductor look exactly the same. Perhaps they're twins.

Head One ⎱ No, Head Three. They don't look the same.　⎰ *Speaking*
Head Two ⎰ They *are* the same. Same man, different hat.⎱ *together*

Conductor That's right! The bus company can only afford to pay one person, so I have to do both jobs. But I can't do both jobs at the same time, so I have one hat per job to remind me who I am. (*He puts the driver's hat on*) All aboard! (*He puts the conductor's hat on*) Any more fares, please!

Head Three I see.

Conductor Now, come on, I can't stand around here chatting all day. The driver's waiting to go. (*He puts on the driver's hat*) That's right. (*He puts on the conductor's hat*) Do you want a ticket?

Head Three How much?

Conductor Five pence.

Head Three Five.

Conductor Per head.

All Heads What?

Conductor That's fifteen pence.

All Heads But I only want one ticket. I am one creature.

Conductor Can't help that—the rules say five pence a head, and I can see three heads.

All Heads Of course, because I am the Three-Headed Knowall.

Conductor Fifteen pence, please.

All Heads Certainly not. (*Exiting*) How dare he. Never heard anything like it. What a nerve, etc.

> *The Three-Headed Knowall exits.*
> *Mr and Mrs Silly Cuckoo enter*

Conductor Time to go, chum. (*He changes to the driver's hat*) Right, mate!

The Bus Driver starts to get into his cab.

Mrs Silly Cuckoo Oh look, the bussywuss!

Mr Silly Cuckoo Oh Mrs Silly Cuckoo—let's go for a drivywive.

Mrs Silly Cuckoo Betterwetter still, let's go to townywowny.

Mr Silly Cuckoo What for?

Mrs Silly Cuckoo To look for a conductorwuctor. (*She gestures like a conductor*)

Mr Silly Cuckoo Of course!

They hurry to the bus

Mrs Silly Cuckoo (*to the Bus Driver*) Two tickiwickets to townywowny, please.

Bus Driver Don't ask me. *I'm* the driver. Ask the conductor.

Mrs Silly Cuckoo Right.

Mr and Mrs Silly Cuckoo hurry to the entrance. Mrs Silly Cuckoo stops halfway in sudden realization, and Mr Silly Cuckoo bumps into her

What did he say?

Mr Silly Cuckoo (*without having caught on*) He said, "Don't ask me! *I'm* the driver. Ask the conductor."

He realizes, and they look wide-eyed at each other

Mr Silly Cuckoo } The conductorwuctor! { *Speaking*
Mrs Silly Cuckoo } { *together*

Giggling, they advance to the entrance. The Bus Driver, who has changed hats, comes to meet them

Conductor Any more fares, please?
Mrs Silly Cuckoo Are you a conductor——
Mr Silly Cuckoo—wuctor?
Conductor (*looking at his hat quickly to check*) Er—that's right.
Mr Silly Cuckoo } (*grabbing the Conductor and pulling* { *Speaking*
Mrs Silly Cuckoo } *him off the bus*) Wheeeeee!! { *together*
Conductor 'Ere, what's going on? Put me down!
Mrs Silly Cuckoo Conduct us, please . . .
Mr Silly Cuckoo Please conduct us, make us sing togetherwether!
Conductor What?

Mr and Mrs Silly Cuckoo sing their "Cuckoos" and "Oo-cucks" at the bewildered Conductor, who shrugs his shoulders and raises his hands in a gesture of amazement. Seeing him raise his arms like the Penguin did when demonstrating earlier, Mr and Mrs Silly Cuckoo get even more eager

Mrs Silly Cuckoo Yes, yes, he's doing it, lookywook! Cuckoo, cuckoo.
Mr Silly Cuckoo That's it, that's it! Oo-cuck, oo-cuck.
Conductor (*loudly*) I think you're both barmy.

Mr and Mrs Silly Cuckoo hear this and quieten down immediately

Mrs Silly Cuckoo What did he say?
Mr Silly Cuckoo He said we were . . .
Conductor *Barmy.*
Mrs Silly Cuckoo *You're* the barmy-warmy one.
Mr Silly Cuckoo Fancy a conductorwuctor who can't conductiwuct!
Conductor (*if the audience have not by now shouted out that they've got the wrong sort of conductor*) But I'm a *bus* conductor—I can't conduct silly singing cuckoos.
Mr Silly Cuckoo } Oh. { *Speaking*
Mrs Silly Cuckoo } { *together*
Mrs Silly Cuckoo Why didn't you say so?
Mr Silly Cuckoo Making us look sillybillywillies.
Mrs Silly Cuckoo Come along, Mr Silly Cuckoo, let's get on the bussy-wussy. (*She gives the Conductor money*)
Mr Silly Cuckoo Yes, Mrs Silly Cuckoo, perhaps we'll find a *proper* (*looking at the Conductor*) conductor in townywowny.

The Conductor gives them their tickets, rings the bell, changes his hat, and becomes the Driver

SONG: COME FOR A RIDE (Reprise)

Mr Silly Cuckoo
Mrs Silly Cuckoo

Come let us ride
In this beautiful bus
Travel in comfort
No trouble or fuss
Let's have a treat
Let's take a seat
Let us board
This beautiful bus.

Singing together

Bus Driver
Mr Silly Cuckoo
Mrs Silly Cuckoo

Less dangerous than a spaceship
A yacht can go off course
Smoother than ice skating
Comfier than a horse
Less bumpy than a camel
More spacious than a van
Safer than to try to
Fly like Peter Pan . . .

Come for a/Let us ride
In my/This beautiful bus
Travel in comfort
No trouble, no fuss
Come for a/Let's have a treat
Come take/Let's take a seat
All Aboard/Let us board
My/This beautiful bus.

Singing together

The bus moves off

Flibberty and the Penguin rush on

Flibberty Hey, wait for us! Come on, Percival . . .

The Penguin is not able to move fast enough

Quick. (*To the bus*) Please wait!

Too late, the bus has gone

Oh no, we'll have to flibberty walk. Let's have a rest first.

The Penguin gestures off the way they came

What is it? (*Helped by the audience*) Oh yes, of course— Krafty King-fisher. Well, don't worry, he's nowhere in sight. Perhaps he's given up. You go to sleep.

The Penguin is nervous and mimes "Why not ask the audience to help by watching out for Krafty Kingfisher for them?"

What? Ask them to keep a look-out for him? (*To the audience*) Would you do that? Shout out "Krafty Kingfisher" if you see him? Oh, thank you. There you are, Percival—we'll be quite safe. Now, you sleep over there. (*He points to the mound where the bus stop stands*) I'll keep guard.

The Penguin lies down and goes to sleep. Flibberty patrols downstage, humming the Penguin song

Krafty Kingfisher enters upstage

Audience reaction. Krafty Kingfisher sees Flibberty, who is asking the audience where the Krafty Kingfisher is. Krafty Kingfisher advances and goes to jump on Flibberty who, at the crucial moment, moves away, leaving Krafty Kingfisher to fall on the ground cursing. Flibberty crosses to the other side of the stage, still searching. Krafty Kingfisher gets up and follows him over. As before, Krafty Kingfisher pounces just as Flibberty moves, and Krafty Kingfisher falls on the ground again. This time, as he gets up he spots the Penguin asleep. This is his real objective, so he starts advancing towards the Penguin. The audience are still shouting. Flibberty turns to see the situation just as Krafty Kingfisher raises his beak in a terrifying manner for the painful, poisonous, paralysing peck. He runs to the Penguin, pushes him so that he rolls over and over, just as Krafty Kingfisher's beak descends and goes straight into the grass and earth, where it is embedded and he is stuck. The Penguin, of course, wakes up

Flibberty quickly drags the Penguin off

Kingfisher Ahhhh! Bejubejubejubejub. (*Eventually he frees himself*) You'll suffer for this, Penguin—and *you*, Flibberty—(*to the audience*)—and you —oooh my poor beak, it's all sore! But you wait. Krafty Kingfisher isn't finished yet!

SONG: PECK THAT PENGUIN

(*Singing*)   I'm going to
                         Poisonously peck that Penguin
                         Paralyse him with my sting
                         Poisonously peck that Penguin
                         Teach him that I'm the king
                         The king Kingfisher
                         The Krafty Kingfisher
                         Nobody is craftier than me
                         See? I'll
                         Poisonously peck that Penguin
                         I'll pay him back for pinching my tea.

                         No mercy, I'll
                         Poisonously peck that Penguin

Peck him till his eardrums ring
Poisonously peck that Penguin
Teach him that I'm the king
The king Kingfisher
The Krafty Kingfisher
No-one is more craftier, that's true
Phew! I'll
Poisonously peck that Penguin
And if I don't peck him I'll peck you!

He points at the audience

And you, and you, and you!
Yes, if I don't peck him I'll peck you!

The Krafty Kingfisher exits

SCENE 4

The town.

We see a street with a Police Station with a door, and a lamp outside, a Bus Stop and the Stage Door of the Colossal Concert Hall. On a wall there is a large poster advertising a Grand Concert to celebrate the first day of spring. The large choir is to be conducted by Mr Maestro, the celebrated conductor. On the poster is a large picture of him in full evening dress—looking somewhat similar to the Penguin

The Policeman enters on a scooter. He wears spectacles and he is happy, humming to himself—but not very tunefully. We hear odd phrases like "Spring is in the air", etc. He stops outside the Police Station

Policeman Heigh-ho. Spring will soon be here. (*He gets off and leaves his scooter against the wall*) Good riddance, winter. Hurry up, spring. (*Seeing the lamp*) Hallo hallo, this lamp looks dirty. (*He touches it*) P'raps it's time for a spring clean.

The Policeman goes into the Station, humming.
Master Ministrone enters. He is not very tall and, like his master Mr Maestro, has an Italian accent. He carries a huge suitcase with Mr Maestro written on it in large letters. He staggers under the weight and we can hardly see his face hidden under it. He reaches the edge of the stage, nearly falls off, but changes direction just in time.
The Policeman emerges from the Police Station, putting on an apron over his uniform. He starts polishing the lamp with a feather duster and standing with his back to Master Ministrone who, unable to see where he is going, bumps into him and drops the suitcase

Policeman Oi! What's going on?

Ministrone I'm a-so sorry. Please-a forgive me, lady, please-a forgive.

Policeman Lady? What do you mean, lady?

Ministrone Oh. I'm-a-so sorry. You weara ze apron like-a ze lady. I thought . . .

Policeman I'm not a lady, I'm a policeman.

Ministrone Oh. I'm a-so sorry.

Policeman There's no need to be. I quite enjoy it. I'm wearing an apron because I'm spring cleaning. Spring is nearly here, you know.

Ministrone Si si, that is-a why I am here.

Policeman What, to do my spring cleaning?

Ministrone No, to, to-a celebrate the arrival of spring! In song.

Policeman Oh! (*Pointing to the poster*) This, you mean? the grand concert?

Ministrone (*seeing the poster*) That's-a right. (*Picking up the suitcase*) I must-a take this in the stage-a door.

Policeman (*seeing the name on the suitcase*) Mr Maestro the famous conductor?

Ministrone Si, si.

Policeman But you're not Mr Maestro, are you? You look nothing like his picture up there. Wait a minute. Have you stolen his suitcase?

Ministrone No, no, no—I am-a Mr Maestro's assistant—Master Ministrone.

Master Ministrone takes the suitcase off through the stage door

Policeman Master Ministrone? (*Returning to his work*) What a funny name.

Maestro (*off, singing*) Master Ministrone! Master Ministrone!

Policeman (*looking off*) Oh, *that* looks like Mr Maestro. (*To the audience*) He's *very* famous, you know. (*Remembering the apron*) I'd better take this off. (*He does so, hiding the duster, and stands to attention*)

Mr Maestro enters. He wears evening dress, as in the poster, but also top hat, gloves and a large coat or cloak. He carries a small case

Maestro (*singing*) Master Ministrone, have we-a time before the concert to practise? Master Ministrone! Where are-a you?

Policeman (*putting on a posh voice*) Excuse me, sir, Master Ministrone has conveyed your case into the Concert Hall.

Mr Maestro only hears or understands people if they sing to him. Therefore he does not hear the Policeman

Maestro (*seeing the Policeman; singing*) Aha! A policeman. Have you seen my assistant?

Policeman Yes, sir, as I said, he has conveyed your . . .

Maestro (*singing*) Why do you-a not answer my question?

Policeman But sir, I did! Master Ministrone . . .

Maestro (*singing*) Oh. It's-a useless. I will have to search-a myself. Master Ministrone! (*To the Policeman*) What is-a the time?

Policeman (*looking at his watch*) Exactly a quarter to three sir.
Maestro Stupid man. What is-a the time? (*Sarcastically*) If you want-a to know the time ask a policeman. Ha, ha, ha.
Policeman (*thinking Mr Maestro is deaf, and shouting*) A quarter to three.
Maestro (*singing in a passionate state*) The time! What is-a the time?
Policeman (*in a louder voice*) I've told you. A quarter . . .
Maestro (*singing*) The time!!

Master Ministrone enters from the Stage Door carrying a large music score

What is-a the time?
Ministrone (*to the Policeman*) Excuse me, what is-a the time?
Policeman (*exasperated*) A quarter to three.
Ministrone (*singing to Mr Maestro*) A quarter to three.
Maestro (*immediately calm*) Good. Good. I have-a time to practise.
Ministrone (*singing*) Yes, Mr Maestro, a-plenty.

Mr Maestro puts down his case and starts grandly to remove his gloves, hat and cloak, handing each article to Master Ministrone while singing a scale

Policeman (*to Ministrone, whispering*) Psst. Why did he understand you and not me?
Ministrone (*collecting the gloves*) Did you speak to him?
Policeman Yes.
Ministrone Ah! He-a only understands-a if you sing to him.

Mr Maestro jams his hat down on Master Ministrone's head—right over his eyes

Policeman Only understands singing? Funny fellow.

The Policeman scratches his head and goes into the Police Station

Mr Maestro, still singing a scale, removes the cloak and tosses it on Master Ministrone, enveloping him

Maestro (*singing*) Now, give-a me my-a baton and-a my-a spectacles.
Ministrone (*singing, muffled under the cloak*) Where are they?
Maestro (*singing*) In-a my case.
Ministrone Ah. (*Still enveloped, he walks and trips over the case*)
Maestro (*singing*) Ahh! Attentione! Don't break my-a spectacles.

Master Ministrone gets up, manages to take off the cloak, and puts it on himself

Ministrone (*singing*) Here you are, Mr Maestro. (*He opens the case and produces a large baton*) Your baton!
Maestro (*taking it, singing*) Aha! La la la la la la . . . (*He sings a fast, complicated tune, which he conducts frenetically, rather like a fencer having a work-out before a match. Singing*) Spectacles.
Ministrone (*singing*) Si, si, Mr Maestro. (*He turns to look in the case. As he bends over he is prodded by the baton as it is waved. He jumps, says "Ow",*

looks round, by which time the baton is being waved high in the air again)
That's-a funny. (*The business is repeated*) A-very funny. (*The business is
repeated again. The audience may be shouting to tell him what is happening.
This time he feels what prods him, grasps it and, without seeing Mr Maestro,
feels up the baton, up Mr Maestro's arm, then comes face to face with
Mr Maestro. Screaming*) Ahahh!

Maestro (*singing*) What are you a-doing?

Ministrone (*singing*) Your baton was a-prodding me.

Maestro I'm a-sorry. Now—(*impatiently*)—where are my-a spectacles?

Ministrone (*turning back to the suitcase*) Which-a ones do you want? These?
(*He hands over a pair with very large, heavy frames*)

Maestro (*putting them on and singing in a deep, very loud voice*) No, no, these
are much-a too large. Something smaller. (*He takes them off and gives
them back*)

Ministrone (*taking the large glasses and giving him a small pair of steel-
rimmed ones*) Try these, Mr Maestro.

Maestro (*putting them on and singing in a very high, small, prim voice*) No,
no, these are much-a too small. Something in-a the middle.

Ministrone (*taking them back and handing over a more normal pair*) These
are your-a short-sighted spectacles.

Maestro (*putting them on and singing*) Ah, that is-a better. Where is-a the
music?

Ministrone (*picking up the score and holding it against his chest*) Here we are,
Mr Maestro.

Maestro (*singing*) Where, where? I cannot-a see it!

Ministrone (*singing*) Come a-closer. They are short-sighted spectacles.

Maestro (*advancing*) Ah!

Ministrone (*singing*) Closer, closer, closer.

Mr Maestro arrives, nose pressed up to the score

Is that-a all right?

Maestro (*singing*) No, no, no, it's-a hopeless.

Ministrone (*singing*) Perhaps you had-a better try your long-sighted spectacles instead. (*He puts down the score, takes Mr Maestro's short-sighted
spectacles off him, and collects another pair from the case*) Here you are.

Maestro (*singing*) Ah, that is-a better. Now, hold up-a the music.

Ministrone (*singing*) Here it is. (*He holds it up very close to Mr Maestro*)

Maestro (*singing*) No, no, no, further back. These-a are my long-a-sighted
spectacles. Further back.

Master Ministrone starts backing away

(*Louder and louder*) Back. More. More, back, etc.

*Master Ministrone exits backwards, with Mr Maestro still singing after him.
The Policeman enters*

Policeman Hey, hey, what's all this noise? (*He goes to Mr Maestro*) What's
going on?

Maestro (*singing*) More, more, back further, etc.
Policeman (*remembering*) Oh, of course, he only understands singing. Er—
(*singing in a cracked voice*) What is all this noise?
Maestro (*singing*) I cannot see-a my music!
Policeman (*singing*) Where is it?
Maestro (*singing*) Over there. Back, more, more . . . !
Policeman (*singing*) I can't see it.
Maestro (*singing*) I have-a my long-a-sighted spectacles on!
Policeman Ah. I see.

*Master Ministrone enters the other side, still walking backwards, holding
the score. Mr Maestro and the Policeman, of course, do not see him—they
are looking off the side he exited*

Maestro (*singing*) Back, back! More, more!

*Master Ministrone backs into the Policeman, who concertinas into Mr Maes-
tro. All jump violently*

Ah! (*To the Policeman*) How-a dare you! (*He sees Master Ministrone*) Ah,
it was you, was it? I'll a-deal with you later. Now. (*Angrily*) How am I-a
going to practise? I cannot even see-a the music.
Policeman (*singing*) Excuse me, sir—would you like to borrow my spectacles?
Maestro (*singing*) Oh! Si, si. Thank you! Gracie. (*He tries the Policeman's
spectacles on, giving the other pair to Master Ministrone*) Hold up-a the
music.

Master Ministrone holds up the score

Ah! Perfectissimo. (*He shakes hands with the Policeman*) Gracie, gracie!
Policeman (*singing*) Not at all!
Maestro (*charmed*) You-a sing very nicely. How wonderful to find a police-
man who understands music.
Policeman (*singing proudly*) Well, my singing isn't much, but I have had
lessons on the policeman's whistle. (*He gets out his whistle*)
Maestro The policeman's whistle?
Policeman Yes. (*He shows it*)
Maestro Ah! Bellissimo!

SONG: MUSIC IS MAGIC

Maestro ⎫
Ministrone ⎬   ⎱ *Singing*
Policeman ⎭ (*who also uses his whistle*)   ⎰ *together*

Music is magic
It can weave a magic spell
When you're feeling sad
Music makes you feel well
Music is magic

It has power to entrance
When the music starts
People get up and dance
Feet start to tap
Arms start to swing
Knees start to bend
Voice starts to sing
Yes, music is magic and everywhere
Music is, magic is there.

Music
Tra la la la la la la la la
Music
Tra la la la la la la la la
Music
(Policeman's whistle)
La la la la la la la.

Music is magic
It can weave a magic spell
When you're feeling sad
Music makes you feel well
Music is magic
It has power to entrance
When the music starts
People get up and dance
Feet start to tap
Arms start to swing
Knees start to bend
Voice starts to sing
Yes, music is magic and everywhere
Music is, magic is there.

Maestro (*singing*) Splendid! Splendid! Please, you must-a come and be in
my-a concert (*pointing to the poster*) tonight.
Policeman (*very flattered, singing*) I'd love to, Mr Maestro. Many thanks.
(*He starts to go into the Police Station*)
Maestro (*waving an operatic farewell*) Till tonight, then. Till tonight.
Policeman Cheerio, cheerio!

The Policeman waves, exits and closes the door

*Master Ministrone picks up the case, score, etc., and goes to the Stage Door
to open it for Mr Maestro, who makes an operatic exit*
Maestro Farewell! Farewell!

Mr Maestro and Master Ministrone exit.
    The bus enters with the Silly Cuckoos on board. The Bus Driver brakes

Bus Driver We've arrived in town, Conductor. (*He quickly changes hats*)

Thank you, Driver! Police Station and Concert Hall! Police Station and Concert Hall!

Mrs Silly Cuckoo Let's get off the bussy-wussy here, Mr Silly Cuckoo.

Mr Silly Cuckoo If you say so, Mrs Silly Cuckoo.

Mrs Silly Cuckoo (*getting off the bus*) We can look for a conductorwuctor here.

Mr Silly Cuckoo Yes indeedyweedy.

Mrs Silly Cuckoo Thank you, bus conductor——

Mr Silly Cuckoo—wuctor.

Conductor Thank you, madam, sir.

Mrs Silly Cuckoo Come along, Mr Silly Cuckoo!

The Silly Cuckoos pass the front of the bus. By this time the Conductor has changed hats again and arrived at the driving seat

Mr Silly Cuckoo Thank you, bus driver——

Mrs Silly Cuckoo—wiver.

Bus Driver Thank you, sir, madam.

Mr Silly Cuckoo Come along, Mrs Silly Cuckoo!

Mrs Silly Cuckoo (*seeing the poster on the wall*) Oooh. Looky-wooky.

Mr Silly Cuckoo What is it?

Mrs Silly Cuckoo A posterwoster.

Mr Silly Cuckoo With a picturewicture!

Mrs Silly Cuckoo What does it say?

Mr Silly Cuckoo I don't know. *I* can't readyweady.

Mrs Silly Cuckoo *I* can't eitherweither.

Mr Silly Cuckoo ⎫
Mrs Silly Cuckoo ⎬ We *both* can't readyweady . . . ⎰ *Speaking*
                                                        ⎱ *together*

If the audience hasn't already offered to read it, Mr Silly Cuckoo asks them to help

Audience "GRAND CONCERT TO CELEBRATE ARRIVAL OF SPRING. HUNDREDS OF SINGERS. MR MAESTRO 'CONDUCTOR'."

Mr Silly Cuckoo ⎫
Mrs Silly Cuckoo ⎬ Conductorwuctor? Conductorwuctor?

Audience Yes!

Mr Silly Cuckoo That's what we are lookywooking for.

Mrs Silly Cuckoo Come on, Mr Silly Cuckoo, He can't be far away.

The Silly Cuckoos exit hurriedly

Bus Driver All aboard. All aboard. Bus station next stop. (*He changes hats to the Conductor*) Any more fares, please? (*He rings the bell and goes back to the driving seat, changing hats*)

Mr Maestro and Master Ministrone enter from the Stage Door

Maestro (*singing*) Come along, Master Ministrone, exercise time. Must-a be fit for the concert.

They stand in the path of the bus and begin to do deep breathing exercises and physical jerks. Master Ministrone counts to beat time

Ministrone (*singing*) A-one, a-two, a-three, a-four. A-one, etc.

Bus Driver (*sitting ready to take off, and seeing Mr Maestro and Master Ministrone in his path*) 'Allo. What's this? Conductor, there's an obstruction in the road. Kindly remove it. (*He dashes back, changing hats, gets off the bus, and goes up to the others*)

Mr Maestro and Master Ministrone are doing their exercises—arms up, down, out, etc.

Conductor Would you mind standing clear? My bus cannot pass.

Mr Maestro, unaware of the interruption, is just doing an "arms out" movement, which knocks off the Conductor's hat

How dare you! (*He picks up his hat and goes round to the other side to speak to Master Ministrone*)

Master Ministrone stops his exercises to talk to the Conductor

'Ere, Shorty!

Ministrone (*speaking*) A-what do you want?

Conductor Please budge.

Ministrone Budge?

Conductor Scarper, vamoose.

Maestro (*to Master Ministrone, singing*) Why are you not a-counting?

Ministrone (*to Mr Maestro, singing*) This-a man says scarper, vamoose.

Maestro (*singing*) Why?

Ministrone (*to the Conductor, speaking*) Why?

Conductor You're in the bus's way.

Ministrone (*to Mr Maestro, singing*) We're in the bus's way.

Maestro (*singing*) What a cheek. Who does he-a think he is?

Ministrone (*to the Conductor, speaking*) Who do you-a think you are?

Conductor (*checking his hat*) The Conductor.

Ministrone (*To Mr Maestro, singing*) The Conductor!

Maestro (*singing*) What?

Ministrone (*singing*) The Conductor!

Maestro (*furiously, singing*) *I'm* the Conductor!

Ministrone (*to the Conductor, shouting*) He's the Conductor.

Conductor No, he's not.

Ministrone (*to Mr Maestro, singing*) No, you're not.

Maestro (*now furious with Master Ministrone*) Of course I am.

Ministrone (*singing*) I *know* you are.

Maestro (*singing*) How-a dare you.

Ministrone (*singing*) *He* says you're not.

As a row breaks out between Mr Maestro and Master Ministrone the Conductor shrugs his shoulders and returns to the bus

Maestro (*beginning to sob*) You-a hurt-a my feelings.

Ministrone I didn't mean-a to . . .
Maestro (*with a huge gesture*) Ah! (*He goes into a huff*)

Master Ministrone, seeing the bus about to depart, tries to pull Mr Maestro away, but he refuses to budge

Conductor Drive on, driver. If they won't move themselves, we'll do it for them. (*He rings the bell several times, then changes hats and returns to the driving seat*)

The Maestro hears the bell and breaks out of his huff

Maestro (*singing*) Ah! What-a was that? That-a music, soothing music!
Ministrone (*singing*) The bus bell.
Maestro (*singing*) What a beautiful sound! (*He rushes up to the bus, which is about to move*)
Bus Driver Off we go, then.
Maestro (*singing*) Please-a stop! Ring-a your bell again.
Bus Driver I can't, I'm sorry. It's not my job.
Ministrone (*to Mr Maestro, singing*) It's not his job.
Maestro (*singing*) Who is he?
Ministrone (*to the Bus Driver, speaking*) Who are you?
Bus Driver I'm the driver.
Ministrone (*to Mr Maestro, singing*) He's the driver.
Maestro (*singing*) Please-a bring your bus to my-a concert tonight.
Bus Driver (*driving off*) All right, but what for?
Ministrone (*to Mr Maestro, singing*) All right, but what for?
Maestro (*singing*) So we can year the music of the bell.
Bus Driver I'll have to ask the Conductor. (*He changes hats and discusses it with himself*)
Maestro (*singing*) Ah, the bella bella bella bell!

SONG: WHAT A BELLA BELLA BELL!

Maestro (*singing*)
I've spent a lifetime in music
But today I'm in luck for
I've never heard a sound so crystal clear
As the noise made by this Conductor
When he presses this little button here!

Maestro
Ministrone
] Wella wella well
What a bella bella bell
Ting a ling a ling
Ting a ling a ling a ling
Sing a sing a sing
What a ring a ding a ding
Ting a ling a ling a
What a bella bella bell. [*Singing together*

By this time the Bus Conductor has shown enthusiasm and presses the bell. The next verse is sung as a round, the first part being taken by Mr Maestro, the second by Master Ministrone, and the third by the Conductor

> Wella wella well
> What a bella bella bell
> Ting a ling a ling
> Ting a ling a ling a ling
> Sing a sing a sing
> What a ring a ding a ding
> Ting a ling a ling a
> What a bella bella bell.

The Conductor changes hats to drive away

The bus exits, and Mr Maestro and Master Ministrone go off through the Stage door.

Flibberty and the Penguin enter, running

Flibberty Ah. The Police Station! At last! Percival, you stay here. I'll go in and ask if they've seen your mother and father.

The Penguin is alarmed at this suggestion and points off to where he thinks Krafty Kingfisher may be coming in pursuit

What? Krafty Kingfisher? It's all right, he's miles away. I won't be long, anyway.

Flibberty goes into the Police Station

The Penguin looks nervously about. Deciding to risk it, he puts down his suitcase and gingerly sits on it

Krafty Kingfisher enters

Kingfisher Ah! Bejubejubejubejub!

The Penguin sees him, gets up, leaves his suitcase, and chases off. Krafty Kingfisher pursues him.

Mr and Mrs Silly Cuckoo enter

Mrs Silly Cuckoo (*calling*) Conductorwuctor! Conductorwuctor!
Mr Silly Cuckoo Maybe he hasn't arrived yet, Mrs Silly Cuckoo.

Mr Maestro and Master Ministrone enter from the Stage Door

Maestro (*singing hoarsely*) Find a chemist's shop, prestissimo! My voice is a-going.
Ministrone (*singing*) Yes, Mr Maestro—what shall I buy?
Maestro (*singing*) A packet of throat lozenges for-a me to suck! Prestissimo!
Ministrone I'll be as prestissimo as possible!

Master Ministrone exits by the side opposite from where the Silly Cuckoos are watching, excitedly.

Mr Maestro goes back through the Stage Door

Mrs Silly Cuckoo Mr Silly Cuckoo . . .
Mr Silly Cuckoo Yes, Mrs Silly Cuckoo?
Mrs Silly Cuckoo Did you see thatywat?
Mr Silly Cuckoo (*pointing to the poster*) Just like the picturewicture.
Mrs Silly Cuckoo A conductorwuctor! (*To the audience*) It was, wasn't it?
Audience Yes.
Mr Silly Cuckoo Oh, luviwuviduvly! We'll be the first cuckoos of springy-wingy. (*He goes towards the Stage Door*) Let's ask him now.
Mrs Silly Cuckoo Let's make ourselves look beautiweautiful first.

The Silly Cuckoos face each other fussily, smartening each other

The Penguin enters, running away from Krafty Kingfisher. In his panic he goes through the Stage Door to hide.

Krafty Kingfisher enters in pursuit, passes the Stage Door, and chases off the other side

The Silly Cuckoos have not seen this episode, and now prepare to meet Mr Maestro

Mrs Silly Cuckoo (*calling*) Conductorwuctor!

They go to the Stage Door

Mr Silly Cuckoo (*calling*) Conductorwuctor!
Mrs Silly Cuckoo We want your helpywelp!
Mr Silly Cuckoo I'd better knockywock. (*He goes to knock on the Stage Door*)

At this moment the Penguin emerges, relieved to have avoided Krafty King-fisher. He shuts the door

The Silly Cuckoos mistake the Penguin for Mr Maestro

Mrs Silly Cuckoo Here he isywis! Conductorwuctor!
Mr Silly Cuckoo Please helpywelpy. We want to be the first cuckoos of springywingy.

Mr and Mrs Silly Cuckoo advance on the Penguin, who senses danger and backs away. He bumps into the Policeman's scooter which is leaning against the wall, sees it, and scoots off L, pursued by the Silly Cuckoos

Mrs Silly Cuckoo What's the matterwatter?
Mr Silly Cuckoo Come backywack! Pleaseyweasy!

The Penguin exits L, followed by the Silly Cuckoos.

Krafty Kingfisher enters, realizing that he has missed the Penguin

Kingfisher Ahhh. Bejubejubejubejub! Missed him! (*Calling*) Penguin! He must have hidden somewhere. (*He stalks round, looking*) Where, where, where?

Mr Maestro enters from the Stage Door, carrying his case. He is hoarse, and desperate for his lozenges

Maestro (*singing*) Master Ministrone! Where-a are you? My throat is a-getting worse!

Krafty Kingfisher sees Mr Maestro and mistakes him for the Penguin

Kingfisher Ahhh! There he is. Jubbyjubbyjubbyjubbyjub!

Mr Maestro turns, to see the advancing Krafty Kingfisher

Maestro (*singing*) Who are you? What do you a-want? Help!

Mr Maestro turns and runs off R

Kingfisher Thief! Fishstealer! I'll peck you, peck you, peck, peck, peck.

Krafty Kingfisher exits R *in pursuit. Immediately there is a chase across the stage from* L *to* R: *the Penguin, still on the scooter, pursued by the Silly Cuckoos, calling "Conductorwuctor!" They exit.*

Another chase follows from R *to* L: *Mr Maestro, singing "Help!" is chased by Krafty Kingfisher. They exit.*

Flibberty enters from the Police Station

Flibberty No, I'm sorry, Percival. The Policeman hasn't seen any penguins recently. We'll have to . . . (*He sees the Penguin is not there*) Percival! Where are you? (*To the audience*) Have you seen him?

The audience shout out that the Silly Cuckoos are chasing him

As Flibberty gets the message, the Penguin scoots on from R *to* L *pursued by the Silly Cuckoos. Flibberty jumps out of the way just in time and, realizing what has happened, chases off* L *after them.*

Master Ministrone enters R *with the throat lozenges*

Ministrone (*singing*) Mr Maestro! Mr Maestro! I've-a got them!

Master Ministrone goes into the Stage Door. At the same moment Mr Maestro enters, chased from L *to* R *by Krafty Kingfisher*

Maestro (*singing*) Help! Help!

Kingfisher I'll teach you to steal my fish.

Mr Maestro and Krafty Kingfisher exit R. Master Ministrone comes out of the Stage Door

Ministrone I can't-a see Mr Maestro anywhere. (*To the audience*) Have-a you seen him?

The audience shout out that he is being chased by Krafty Kingfisher

Mr Maestro dashes on, chased from R to L by Krafty Kingfisher. Master Ministrone jumps out of the way just in time, realizes what has happened, and chases off L after them.

CHASE: *From L to R the Penguin (on the scooter) is chased by the Silly Cuckoos, who are chased by Flibberty, who is chased by Krafty Kingfisher, yelling "Peck, peck, peck!" Flibberty turns in fright, sees it is Krafty Kingfisher and reacts terrified, running off R. Krafty Kingfisher stops in surprise, having seen Flibberty and Mr Maestro, followed by Master Ministrone, both concertina into him, almost knocking him over—he turns, sees Mr Maestro and, still taking him for the Penguin, chases him L, thus forcing Master Ministrone to turn to L in front of them*

Master Ministrone does not exit L, but turns round and starts back towards C. Mr Maestro and Krafty Kingfisher follow him

At the same moment, from R, Flibberty runs on, followed by the Penguin pursued by the Silly Cuckoos

Master Ministrone and Flibberty meet C, collide and fall over as the others rush past. They get up and look around, but everyone else has exited

In the confusion each dashes off the wrong way: Flibberty goes off R after Mr Maestro and Krafty Kingfisher; Master Ministrone goes off L after the Penguin and the Silly Cuckoos.

The Penguin enters L. He is caught by the Silly Cuckoos

Mrs Silly Cuckoo What a silly fussywuss, conductorwuctor.
Mr Silly Cuckoo All we want you to do is conductywuct us.

The Penguin tries to mime that he cannot

Mrs Silly Cuckoo Listen. Oo-cuck! Oo-cuck!
Mr Silly Cuckoo (*with the wrong notes again*) Cuckoo, cuckoo.
Mrs Silly Cuckoo Make us sing togetherwether.

The Penguin lifts his arms in desperation, and Mr and Mrs Silly Cuckoo think he is conducting

Mr Silly Cuckoo That's it. That's it. Cuckoo, cuckoo!
Mrs Silly Cuckoo Oo-cuck, oo-cuck!

They carry on trying

Mr Maestro enters R *and is caught by Krafty Kingfisher*

The Penguin and the Silly Cuckoos freeze

Kingfisher Ahh. Jubbyjubbyjubbyjub! Now, Penguin . . .
Maestro (*singing*) Mercy. (*He goes on his knees*) Mercy. What have-a I done?
Kingfisher You know very well what. You stole my fish!
Maestro (*singing, not able to understand*) Mercy, mercy.
Kingfisher (*grabbing Mr Maestro's case*) It's in here. (*He opens the case*) See!

There is nothing in the case but the baton

Ahhh! You've eaten it. (*He breaks the baton in half*)
Maestro (*singing*) Ah. My baton. (*He weeps pitifully*)
Kingfisher Stop crying, Penguin. Don't be weedy. Get ready for a painful, poisonous, paralysing peck.

Krafty Kingfisher and Mr Maestro freeze as the Penguin and the Silly Cuckoos "come back to life" and carry on with their "oo-cucks", etc.

Master Ministrone enters L: *thinking the Penguin is Mr Maestro he runs up and tries to pull him away from Mr and Mrs Silly Cuckoo*

Ministrone Let-a Mr Maestro go! He will be in no fit state-a for the concert.
Mrs Silly Cuckoo (*holding on to the Penguin*) Certainly notywot.
Mr Silly Cuckoo He's teaching us to sing togetherwether.
Ministrone (*singing*) Don't-a worry, Mr Maestro—I'll-a save you.

The Penguin looks even more bewildered as he is pulled this way and that. Then Mr and Mrs Silly Cuckoo, the Penguin and Master Ministrone freeze as Mr Maestro and Krafty Kingfisher "come back to life" and take up where they left off

Maestro (*singing*) Mercy, mercy.
Kingfisher (*getting ready for the big peck*) Ahhhhh. . . .

Flibberty enters R *in the nick of time and, thinking Mr Maestro is the Penguin, goes to pull him away from Krafty Kingfisher*

Flibberty Unhand this penguin! (*He pulls Mr Maestro off his knees*)
Kingfisher Ah. Flibberty! Bejubejubejubejub. Out of my way.
Flibberty Certainly not. (*To Mr Maestro*) It's all right, Percival—he won't peck you.

Mr Maestro looks even more bewildered. Mr and Mrs Silly Cuckoo, the Penguin and Master Ministrone "come to life" again and the two groups' rows

*build with them all shouting at one another. The Penguin and Mr Maestro are
pulled back and forth*

The bus enters, going back to the forest.

*Because everyone is arguing in the road, they do not see the bus, which cannot
get by. The Bus Driver shouts in vain above the hubbub*

Bus Driver Out of my way! Budge! Scarper, etc. (*He eventually gives up,
changes hats, and gets off the bus as the Conductor*)
Conductor (*coming* C) Please clear the road! Let the bus pass, etc.

Noise and pandemonium

*The Policeman enters from the Police Station. He is in his spring-cleaning
apron and carries his feather duster. However, he is putting on his helmet to
preserve a bit of dignity*

Policeman (*shouting*) What's all this noise? Be QUIET!

*No reaction. The Policeman takes out his whistle and blows hard. Everyone is
surprised into a frozen silence. Suddenly the Policeman sees the Penguin on his
scooter*

Who's that on my scooter? Mr Maestro! Only been here half a day and
you're pinching scooters? Oh, sorry. (*He sings*) Mr Maestro, what are you
doing on my scooter?

There is a frozen picture, with the Penguin terrified, as—

THE CURTAIN FALLS

ACT II

SCENE 1

Still in the town

The Curtain rises on the same characters in the same position as at the end of Act I

Policeman (*to the Penguin, thinking he is Mr Maestro*) Well, what have you got to say for yourself?

The Penguin shakes with fear

Speak up, Mr Maestro. (*Realizing he will have to sing*) Oh, I'm sorry. (*Singing*) Mr Maestro, what are you doing on my scooter?
Maestro (*singing*) But, *I* am Mr Maestro!
All What? I thought *he* was Mr Maestro. We've got the wrong one. Who are you then? etc.

The Policeman blows his whistle and all are silent

SONG: COUNT UP TO TEN

Policeman (*singing*) One of the things a policeman
Has to learn to do
Is never to lose his temper
And the same applies to you—
Listen

Squeeze your nose
Close your eyes
Cross your legs and then
Take a deep breath and
Count up to ten—

He takes a deep breath

One, two, three, four, five, six,
Seven, eight, nine, ten.
If your temper's still there, then
Do it again.

The music continues as the Policeman speaks

Now come along, all of you. (*To the audience*) You too. Follow me. (*He sings*)

> Squeeze your nose
> Close your eyes
> Cross your legs and then
> Take a deep breath and
> Count up to ten—

He takes a deep breath

> One, two, three, four, five, six,
> Seven, eight, nine, ten.
> If your temper's still there, then
> Do it again.

The music continues as the Policeman speaks

Once more, and then you'll be as calm as a spring morning.

> Squeeze your nose
> Close your eyes
> Cross your legs and then
> Take a deep breath and
> Count up to ten.

He takes a deep breath

> One, two, three, four, five, six,
> Seven, eight, nine, ten.

(*Speaking*) That's better. Now, what's going on? (*To the Penguin*) Why are you disguised as Mr Maestro?

Flibberty He's not, sir. He's my friend Percival the Penguin. He always looks like that.

Conductor What was all the noise and fuss about? I couldn't get my bus through.

Ministrone Well, I thought that Penguin was Mr Maestro.

Mr Silly Cuckoo ⎱ So did we! ⎰ *Speaking*
Mrs Silly Cuckoo ⎰   ⎱ *together*

Mrs Silly Cuckoo We wanted him to conduct us.

Mr Silly Cuckoo We want to be the first cuckoos of springwingy.

Policeman I see. Well, let's ask him. Mr Maestro, would you . . . (*He remembers, and sings*) Would you conduct the Silly Cuckoos?

Mr Silly Cuckoo ⎱ (*very badly and out of tune*) Please, ⎰ *Singing*
Mrs Silly Cuckoo ⎰ conductorwuctor. We want to be the ⎱ *together*
⎰ first cuckoos of springywingy.

Maestro (*wincing*) Certainly I-a teach you! You-a need it!

Silly Cuckoos Oh. Thank you.

Ministrone (*singing*) Here are your lozenges, Mr Maestro!

Maestro (*singing*) Gracie, gracie. Thank you! But a-look at my baton— a-broken in half! (*He weeps*)

Ministrone (*singing*) How did that happen? We didn't-a bring another one.

The Penguin taps Mr Maestro on the shoulder

Maestro (*singing*) Yes?

The Penguin opens his case and brings out his toothbrush. He offers it to Mr Maestro

A-what is it?

Flibberty (*starting to speak, then singing*) Percival's toothbrush. He's offering it to you to use as a baton.

Maestro (*singing*) Ah! Gracie, gracie. Thank you, thank you. (*He starts having a practice with it*) Now I am-a so grateful. Will-a you all a-please come to my concert this evening? As-a my guests.

All (*singing*) Thank you, etc.

Maestro (*dramatically pointing at Krafty Kingfisher*) Except *him!* He broke-a my baton. Come, Cuckoos.

Mr Maestro, Master Ministrone, and Mr and Mrs Silly Cuckoo exit through the Stage Door

Policeman (*to Krafty Kingfisher*) Is this true?

The Conductor moves to the bus

Where are you going?

Conductor To my bus, I'm running late as it is.

Policeman You stay here. I may need you as a witness.

The Conductor stays

Did you break Mr Maestro's baton?

Kingfisher No. I never touched his rotten baton.

Policeman I think you did. (*To the audience*) Did he break it?

Audience participation

I thought as much.

Kingfisher Ah. Bejubejubejubejub! I thought he was the Penguin anyway.

Policeman What did you want the Penguin for?

Kingfisher He stole my fish.

Policeman (*to the Penguin*) First my scooter, then his fish. Is this true?

The Penguin nods his guilt

Why?

The Penguin mimes hunger

Flibberty He was hungry, sir. He asked Krafty Kingfisher for a fish and he said, "No, go away". Not a very nice way to treat a stranger in the forest— a stranger with no friends.

Policeman Even so, stealing is a very serious matter.

Kingfisher That's right, Policeman. Lock him up!

Policeman (*to the audience*) What do *you* think? Should I lock him up?

Audience participation

Do you think Krafty Kingfisher was mean not to give him a fish? etc.

Audience participation

Very well. I've decided to let you off fish stealing.

The Penguin looks pleased

But what about my scooter?

The Penguin points at Krafty Kingfisher and mimes running away from him, seeing the scooter, and using it to get away

Krafty Kingfisher was chasing you, and so you took my scooter to get away?
Flibberty But he intended to give it back.
Policeman Did you?

The Penguin nods, and gives back the scooter very graciously

Oh, thank you. Very well, I let you off scooter stealing too. You can go free!
Kingfisher What? Ah! Bejubejubejubejub! That's not fair! (*He goes to peck the Policeman*)
Policeman Ahhhh! Right. (*To the Conductor*) You're my witness. You saw that, didn't you?
Conductor He nearly pecked you.
Policeman (*feeling the place*) You're telling me! (*To Krafty Kingfisher*) You're under arrest for attempted policeman-pecking. (*He hauls Krafty Kingfisher off to the Police Station*) Come on. (*To the others*) See you at the Concert. (*Proudly*) Mr Maestro wants me to play my whistle.

The Policeman exits with Krafty Kingfisher

Flibberty I doubt if *we'll* get to the concert.
Conductor Why? Can't you go?
Flibberty Not unless we can find Percival's mother and father before it starts.
Conductor (*to the Penguin*) Where are they?

The Penguin shrugs his shoulders in despair

(*To Flibberty*) Where did he last see them?
Flibberty Iceland.
Conductor Iceland?

The Penguin nods and starts fanning himself

Flibberty And the nearer spring it gets, the hotter Percival gets. So we must find them soon.
Conductor I know—hop in my bus. I'm going to the Zoo. Why not look there? I've only ever seen a penguin in the Zoo before!

The Penguin looks enthusiastic

Flibberty What do you think, Percival? Yes? All right. (*To the Conductor*)

Thank you very much.

The Penguin and Flibberty board the bus

SONG: IN THE ZOO

Conductor &   There are
Flibberty   Chameleons and camels
(*together*)   Marsupials and mammals

                    Ev'rything from a cow to a cockatoo
                    There's pelicans and pythons
                    And bears and bees and bison
                    In the Zoo, in the Zoo, in the Zoo.

                    There's hip-
                    Popotami and hedgehogs
                    And buffaloes and bullfrogs
                    Ev'rything from a crab to a kangaroo
                    Amphibians, anteaters
                    And chimpanzees and cheetahs
                    In the Zoo, in the Zoo, in the Zoo.

                    Flamingos
                    Dingos
                    Ev'ry animal, insect, fish or bird
                    You've heard
                    Of
                    Baboons
                    Racoons
                    They're all on view
                    For all of you—
                    In the Zoo.

                    There's ducks
                    And duckbilled platypuses
                    And owls and octopuses
                    Surely there'll be penguins in there too
                    Your father and your mother
                    May be with one another
                    In the Zoo, in the Zoo, in the Zoo.

                    Your father and your mother
                    May be with one another
                    In the Zoo, in the Zoo, in the Zoo.

SCENE 2

Inside the Police Station

There are a table and chair for the Policeman, a hook on the wall for the cell keys, and the cell itself with a barred door

The Policeman leads Krafty Kingfisher in and takes the keys from the wall

Policeman I'll teach you to try and peck unprotected policemen!
Kingfisher Mind my feathers.
Policeman You mind your manners. (*He opens the cage and pushes Krafty Kingfisher inside*)
Kingfisher Ah! Bejubejubejubejub!
Policeman You'll stay in there till you learn to behave. (*Having locked the door, he hangs the keys on the wall*)
Kingfisher I'm hungry.
Policeman You can stay hungry until teatime. Then I'll give you some tea and toast.
Kingfisher I don't want tea and toast. I want fish. *Fish!* (*He shakes the bars of the cell*)
Policeman Quiet, or you won't get *anything*. Sit down and be good.
Kingfisher Ahh! (*Reluctantly he sits, keeping his eyes on the Policeman*)
Policeman And don't you try to escape either! Now, I'd better have a practice for the concert. (*He gets out his whistle*) Here we are. (*He blows it hard, making the Kingfisher jump*) Or perhaps Mr Maestro would like it soft and romantic. (*He blows it softly*) I wish I could practise with a real tune. (*He has an idea*) *I* know! I'll turn my radio on and join in with an orchestra. (*He switches on the radio*) Now listen to this, Krafty—a taste of real music might do you good.

Over the radio comes the sound of very loud trad jazz. The Policeman looks delighted and joins in, blowing his whistle at irregular intervals and jigging up and down on the spot. Krafty Kingfisher covers his ears and screams

Kingfisher Do I have to listen to that ghastly row?
Policeman (*shouting*) Row? (*He turns off the radio*) It's music.
Kingfisher I don't care what it is. My nerves won't stand it.
Policeman I can't help that. I've got to practise for the concert.
Kingfisher Why not use your headphones?
Policeman My headphones?
Kingfisher Yes. Then *you* can practise and *I* can have a bit of peace.
Policeman Oh. Very well. (*He takes out his headphones*) But I hope no-one needs me for a bit—with these on you can't hear *anything* but the radio. Any other noise can't get through!
Kingfisher Really?
Policeman Yes. (*He puts on the headphones*)
Kingfisher Can't you hear me now, then?
Policeman Let's see. Turn it on!
Kingfisher He can't! Ha, ha, ha! Jubbyjubbyjub!

Having turned the radio on, the Policeman jigs in time with the music, which, of course, we cannot hear. He blows his whistle in so-called time with the music

Right, Policeman. I've spent enough time in here. Krafty by name, crafty by nature. I'll give the Penguin what he deserves if it's the last thing I do!

Music is heard as he assembles his fishing rod and fishes through the bars for the keys on the wall. The Policeman is oblivious to all this, because he is so intent on his music. The audience may scream out to him, but the headphones stop him hearing their warning. Finally Krafty Kingfisher gets the keys and lets himself out

(*Shouting*) Penguin, here I come!

Krafty Kingfisher exits

The Policeman turns off the radio and removes the headphones

Policeman That's enough, I think. I'm nicely warmed up for the concert now—*you* should listen to music, Krafty—it might do you some good. (*He sees Krafty Kingfisher has gone*) Ahh! He's gone! (*He blows his whistle very hard*) Come back, come back!

The Policeman exits

SCENE 3

The Zoo.
There is an archway with "Zoo" written above. A "closed" sign is hanging there, and a bell. We can see cut-out suggestions of a few cages, including a practical one marked "PENGUINS"

The bus arrives with Flibberty, the Penguin and the Bus Driver

SONG: IN THE ZOO

Flibberty &   There's e-
Bus Driver   Mus, elephants and eagles
(*together*)   Bushbabies, bats and beagles
                   Everything from a gnu to a marabou
                   There's tunafish and tortoise
                   And porcupine and porpoise
                   In the Zoo, in the Zoo, in the Zoo.

                   Giraffes
                   And glow worms and gorillas
                   And chickens and chinchillas
                   Surely there'll be penguins in there too
                   Your father and your mother
                   May be with one another
                   In the Zoo, in the Zoo, in the Zoo.

Flibberty Thank you for the ride, Bus Driver.
Bus Driver A pleasure. I'll be waiting outside here. Good luck.
Flibberty Thanks. Come on, Percival.

The Bus Driver parks the bus three-quarters off stage with the entrance in view

Flibberty and the Penguin go to the archway

  Now, who should we ask?

The Penguin points at the bell

  Ring the bell? Good Idea. (*He rings the bell*)

A loud ringing makes them both jump. The Penguin points at the "closed" sign

Flibberty What? Oh dear. Closed.

The Penguin sadly walks away towards the bus

  Percival, don't give up. Someone may be in. (*He rings the bell again*)

The Penguin jumps and stops at a distance from the archway

Zookeeper (*off*) All right. All right. I heard you.

   The Zookeeper enters

  We're closed. Can't you read? Cl—o—s—ed. CLOSED.

Flibberty I know, Zookeeper, but you see it's rather urgent—you see . . .

Zookeeper Come on, come on—hurry up. I'm in the middle of bathing the elephant. He'll catch cold if I hang around chatting to you.

Flibberty Yes, well . . .

Zookeeper Nothing worse than an elephant with a cold. One sneeze and they blow you out of the window. Now, what do you want?

All this time the Penguin remains on the other side of the archway, listening

Flibberty Have you seen any strange penguins recently?

Zookeeper What do you mean—strange? Pink ones with purple spots?

Flibberty No! Strangers—*new* penguins. You see, my friend Percival has lost his mother and father.

Zookeeper What's that got to do with penguins?

Flibberty Well, *he's* a penguin.

Zookeeper Oh. I see! (*A glint comes into his eyes*) You have a friend who's a penguin?

Flibberty Yes. (*He turns*) Percival! (*He sees the Penguin is not next to him*) Oh, hang on a minute. (*He goes to fetch the Penguin from behind the archway*) He's rather shy.

Zookeeper (*to himself*) A penguin! Valuable birds, penguins. Need a new one for the Zoo, too.

Flibberty (*bringing the Penguin in*) Here he is!

Zookeeper (*charmingly*) How do you do, little penguin—my, what a nice fellow you are.

The Zookeeper tickles the Penguin under his chin, which he does not like

Flibberty Well, have you seen them?

Zookeeper What?

Flibberty His parents.

Zookeeper (*examining the Penguin carefully*) No, I don't think so. Do they look like him?

The Penguin escapes from the Zookeeper, grasps Flibberty and mimes to him, pointing to the bus

Flibberty What?

Zookeeper Do his mother and father look like him?

Flibberty Well . . . (*To the Penguin*) What is it, Percival?

The Penguin mimes "the photo in the case"

Of course! The photo—I'll get it. Is it in your case?

The Penguin nods and points to the bus

Flibberty On the bus?

The Penguin nods

Right. Won't be a jiffy. (*He goes to the bus*)

Zookeeper Come here, Penguin.

The Penguin is nervous

Don't be frightened. I just want to look at you closely! (*He does so*) Oh yes! A fine specimen. A very healthy little penguin. I can't wait to—(*he breaks off in time*)—help you find your mother and father.

Flibberty (*entering from the bus with the case*) Here we are. (*He opens the case and takes out the photo, which he shows to the Zookeeper*) Have you seen them?

Zookeeper No. 'Fraid not. But I tell you what.

Flibberty What?

Zookeeper I'll make some enquiries. Some of the animals may well have seen them.

Flibberty Oh, thank you. That's very kind. Isn't it, Percival?

The Penguin nods uncertainly

Zookeeper Would you care to wait in here? (*He opens the door of the cage marked "PENGUINS"*) It's very clean and comfy. You can sit down for a moment.

The Penguin pulls away, and this should help start audience reaction, telling them not to go. The Zookeeper brings out a large key and hides it behind his back

Flibberty Oh, thanks.

The Penguin shakes his head and pulls away

Come on. There's nothing to be afraid of.

Zookeeper No, nothing at all! In you go. I'll be back in a second.

Flibberty Fine. (*He drags the Penguin into the cage*)

Zookeeper Got you! (*He locks the door*) You'll never escape, little penguin, never—you're mine, all mine!

The Zookeeper exits, laughing

Flibberty and the Penguin react terrified; they try to get out but cannot, as the Lights fade

Scene 4

The Concert Hall

The setting is suggested by an ornate music-stand

Master Ministrone is conducting Mr and Mrs Silly Cuckoo

Mr Silly Cuckoo (*singing the wrong notes*) Cuckoo.
Mrs Silly Cuckoo Oo-cuck.
Ministrone No, no, no—you are-a both terrible.
Silly Cuckoos (*to each other*) Terriwerrible! I told you so.
Ministrone It goes like-a this: Cuckoo. (*He sings it correctly*) Cuckoo. Try again. Mrs Silly Cuckoo first.
Mrs Silly Cuckoo Oo-cuck.
Ministrone No, no—Cuck-oo.
Mrs Silly Cuckoo (*with an enormous effort*) Cuck-oo (*Correctly*) Cuckoo, cuckoo.
Ministrone That's-a better. Mr Silly Cuckoo.
Mr Silly Cuckoo (*with the wrong notes*) Cuckoo.
Ministrone No. Cuckoo.
Mr Silly Cuckoo (*tentatively, getting it right*) Cuck-oo. Cuckoo, cuckoo.
Ministrone Bravo! Bravissimo! Very good.
Mr Silly Cuckoo ⎱ Cuckoo, cuckoo, etc. ⎰ *Singing together*
Mrs Silly Cuckoo ⎰   ⎱ *but not in unison*
Ministrone We're nearly ready for-a the concert.

Krafty Kingfisher enters

Kingfisher Ah. Bejubejubejubejub.

Mr and Mrs Silly Cuckoo scatter and hide behind the music-stand with Master Ministrone

Ministrone What-a do you want? You're-a supposed to be in-a prison.
Kingfisher I want that penguin.
Mr Silly Cuckoo We don't knowsywowsy——
Mrs Silly Cuckoo—where he isywis.
Kingfisher If you're telling lies, I'll peck you.
Mr Silly Cuckoo ⎱ No, no, reallyweally, etc. ⎰ *Speaking*
Mrs Silly Cuckoo ⎰   ⎱ *together*
Ministrone Try-a the Zoo. He may have-a gone there.

Kingfisher The Zoo. Right. Penguin, here I come. Ha, ha. Jubbyjubby-jubbyjub.

Krafty Kingfisher exits

Ministrone Right. Quickly. Now we try a deep breathing. In, out, in out, etc.

The Policeman enters on his scooter, blowing his whistle and looking for Krafty Kingfisher

As the Policeman arrives, Master Ministrone has just said "In", so the Silly Cuckoos hold their breath

Policeman Have you seen Krafty Kingfisher? He's escaped.
Ministrone He's-a gone to the Zoo.
Policeman The Zoo? Right. He won't escape me again.

The Policeman exits, blowing his whistle

Ministrone (*seeing the Silly Cuckoos nearly purple*) What's the matter? Oh—out!

The Silly Cuckoos breathe out, relieved

Silly Cuckoos! Now-a we go to the concert.

Master Ministrone and the Silly Cuckoos exit

SCENE 5

The Zoo

The scene opens in darkness to cover the change, the Zookeeper entering downstage to sing his song

SONG: ROLL UP! ROLL UP!

Zookeeper (*singing*)   Roll up! Roll up!
For a treat that's cheap
See my penguin
A penny a peep
Folk will flock from near and far
They will shout Hip Hip Hoorah!
When they see my perfect impeccable
penguin star

During the following chorus the Lights go up on the cage, with the Penguin looking sadly through the bars

I'll feed him well
On fish and such
'Cos I can tell
He likes it so much
I'll keep him spry
And in good shape—
Though he may try
He'll never escape.

Roll up! Roll up!
For a treat that's cheap
See my penguin
A penny a peep
Folk will flock from far and near
They will clap and they will cheer
When they see this perfect impeccable
                              penguin here!

(*Speaking*) Now then, little Penguin, it's nearly your teatime. I won't be long. How about some nice fish? Yes!

The Zookeeper exits.

Flibberty (*calling after him*) What about me? I can't eat raw fish. (*But the Zookeeper has gone*) Oh, Percival, I'm sorry; this is all my flibberty fault.

The Penguin mimes "That's all right"
    You'll never see your mother and father again

The Penguin looks sad

    You may never see Iceland again.

The Penguin begins to sob

    I'm so sorry!

Father and Mother Penguin emerge from the back of the cage

If only *someone* had *seen* your mother and father it would have helped; they could be anywhere, though.

By this time the audience should be telling Flibberty and the Penguin that the Penguin's Father and Mother are behind them

    What? Something behind us?

They look behind, see the Penguins, but do not fully take them in

    How do you do?

Their heads face front again—then suddenly they realize whom they have seen

    Percival—did you see what I saw?

The Penguin nods

They're just like the photograph—are they your . . . ?

The Penguin looks round again, then gets up and runs to his parents in delight. They make a great fuss of him

They are! Percival's mother and father!

All the Penguins come to Flibberty

How do you do? I'm Flibberty.

The Penguin takes his arm and mimes that he is his friend.

Father and Mother Penguin come and show their gratitude to him by patting him heartily on the back with their flippers

(*During this*) We've been looking everywhere for you. Fancy finding you here! Did the Zookeeper catch you too?

Father and Mother Penguin nod, and Father mimes a sack going over Mother's head

In a sack?

Father and Mother Penguin nod

And you've been here ever since?

Father and Mother Penguin nod

Haven't you tried to escape?

Father and Mother Penguin nod and mime that it is impossible

But it can't be impossible.
Kingfisher (*off*) Ah! Bejubejubejubejub!
Flibberty I mean, surely . . .

The Penguin flaps his flippers and looks off nervously. He interrupts and points off. Krafty Kingfisher is approaching

(*Seeing Kingfisher*) Krafty Kingfisher—quick, Penguins, hide!

All three Penguins rush to the back of the cage and turn their backs to the audience

Krafty Kingfisher enters searching for the Penguin

Kingfisher (*crossing*) Bejubejubejubejub. Penguin, where are you? Penguin! Bejubejubejubejub.

Krafty Kingfisher exits on the opposite side

Flibberty (*emerging*) Safe, Penguins. He's gone.

The Penguins turn round and become visible

At the same moment Krafty Kingfisher returns

All the Penguins hide again

Kingfisher (*crossing*) Penguin! Where's my fish? I must have my fish. I'm
starving.

Krafty Kingfisher exits on the opposite side

Once again the Penguins emerge

Flibberty Phew. He wants his fish back, Percival. It's just as well you're
locked in here. He can't peck you.

The Penguin mimes that he does not want to stay here—he wants to escape

What? You don't want to be locked up? Well, I know that, Percival. But
how can we flibberty well escape?

*Depending on the enthusiasm of the audience, it may be possible to discuss
ideas of escape with them—perhaps winning them round to suggesting what in
fact happens in the script! But if not, then the script should be adhered to as
follows*

I've got it!

The Penguins all cluster round

We're locked in here—Percival has a fish in his case. Krafty Kingfisher is
hungry *and* wants to peck Percival. Now, supposing he found out that
Percival is here, what would he do?

*The Penguins mime "Try to get in here", and the audience is encouraged to
interpret this*

Exactly! Try to get in here! Now, how might he get in?

After a moment's thought the Penguins mime "Keys"

Right! He might well steal the keys from the Zookeeper, unlock the door,
and come in—and *we* could be waiting for him! (*To Father Penguin*) When
is the Zookeeper due back?

Father Penguin mimes "Five minutes time—to bring us our supper"

In five minutes time? To bring you your supper? Good. Now, the problem
is, how can we tell Kingfisher that Percival is in here? If he doesn't know
that he'll never even *try* to steal the keys.

The Penguin points to his case and mimes "Smell"

Of course—the fish! If we get the fish out of your case, Percival, Krafty
Kingfisher will smell it, and he'll want to know where it is. Good. But who
can tell him that Percival is in here? Who might he believe?

The audience is encouraged to shout out, "Us!", "We'll tell him", etc.

Would you really? That's marvellous. Let's work it out, then. When
Krafty Kingfisher comes back, he'll smell the fish.

The Penguin gets the fish out of the case and holds it up before putting it down on the floor of the cage

    (*Pointing to the audience*) If he asks you, *you'll* tell him where Percival is. He'll try to get in the cage—but find it locked. So he'll ask how he can get in. *You* can advise him to "wait for Keeper to arrive and steal the keys from him". Then, if the plan works, Krafty Kingfisher will open the cage and go in to look for Percival. Then Percival can knock him over while we all escape.

Everyone looks pleased except the Penguin

    What's the matter, Percival?

The Penguin mimes that he is not very good at fighting

    Oh! Good point. How are we going to overpower Krafty, and escape at the same time?

Pause, then the Penguin holds up his case

    Your case? What about it?

The Penguin points inside the case

    What? Oh, something inside. (*To the audience*) Can you remember what's left inside? (*After allowing the audience to shout it out*) Of course, the bar of soap.

The Penguin mimes putting the soap on the floor and slipping on it.

    That's it! Krafty Kingfisher will slip over—if he's on the floor it will be much easier for us to escape! Good. Now Percival, get out the soap and get ready. We'd better have a quick practice before Krafty Kingfisher comes back. I'll pretend to be Krafty. So, he comes along—smells the fish, and asks where Percival is—now what could you all say?

The audience is encouraged to think of a sentence—such as, "He's inside the cage"

    Fine. "He's inside the cage"—let's all try that together. One, two, three— "*He's inside the cage*". Very good.

If necessary, Flibberty complains that it's not loud enough and to try again, etc.

    Then Krafty Kingfisher will find the cage locked and ask you how to get in. So what could you say in answer to that?

The audience is encouraged to think of a sentence like "Wait for the Zookeeper to arrive, and steal the keys from him"

    Fine—let's all try to say that together. One, two, three—"*Wait for the Zookeeper to arrive and steal the keys from him!*" Very good. Then Krafty Kingfisher will lie in wait; with a bit of luck he'll steal the keys, open the door and slip on the soap—and we can all escape! Now—should we have one more practise?

The whole sequence is rehearsed. As it finishes Krafty Kingfisher is heard approaching

Kingfisher (*off*) Ah. Bejubejubejubejub!

Everyone reacts to this

Flibberty Here he comes! Hide, Penguins.

The Penguins hide

(*To the audience*) Good luck!

Krafty Kingfisher enters

Kingfisher Ah. Bejubejubejubejub. Penguin! I'll find you yet. (*He suddenly sniffs*) What's that lovely smell?

The audience will probably shout out, "Fish"

Fish? So it is. My fish! That means the Penguin must be near here. (*Seeing the audience*) Do *you* know where he is?
Audience He's inside the cage.
Kingfisher Are you certain?
Audience Yes!
Kingfisher Are you to be trusted?
Audience Yes!
Kingfisher Good! So he's in the cage. Right. (*Advancing quietly to the cage*) I'll get him. (*He finds the door locked*)Ahh. Bejubejubejubejub! It's locked. Now, let's see—how can I get in?
Audience Wait for the Zookeeper to arrive and steal the keys from him.
Kingfisher What did you say?
Audience Wait for the Zookeeper to arrive and steal the keys from him.
Kingfisher What a good idea! (*Suddenly*) This isn't a trick, is it?
Audience No.
Kingfisher Are you sure?
Audience Yes.
Kingfisher You'd better be!

The Zookeeper enters with a bucket of fish—supper for the Penguins

(*To the audience, whispering*) Is that him?
Audience Yes!
Kingfisher Right! (*He hides and then pops out to follow the Zookeeper at close range*)

The Penguin lays the soap trap and retreats

Zookeeper Penguins! Pengy pengy Penguins! Here's your supper. (*He takes out the large key and unlocks the door*)

Krafty Kingfisher is behind the Zookeeper, trying to reach the key but unable to do so. The Zookeeper goes in the cage, taking the key with him, and shuts the door. Krafty Kingfisher hides, cross that he has not managed to steal the key. The Penguin suddenly realizes that the Zookeeper might slip on the soap, which would ruin the plan. He rushes out, and in the nick of time retrieves it as the Zookeeper walks by

Here we are. Come and get it! (*He leaves the fish and turns to go*) Eat it while it's fresh and wet. (*He opens the door, goes out, and locks the door*)

Krafty Kingfisher creeps out of hiding and taps the Zookeeper on the shoulder, which makes him turn round. Krafty Kingfisher ducks round and swiftly takes the key out of the lock

What was that? (*He cannot see anything*) Extraordinary! (*He checks the door of the cage is locked, forgets the key, and goes off muttering*) Very odd indeed. Could have sworn someone tapped me on the shoulder.

The Zookeeper exits

Krafty Kingfisher exults and prepares to open the door. The Penguin creeps out of hiding, puts the soap down in a strategic position, and hides once more

Kingfisher (*opening the door*) Aha. Jubbyjubbyjubbyjub. Look out, Penguin, you won't give me the slip again. (*He treads on the soap and slips over*) Aaaaaaah!

Flibberty (*emerging with the Penguin*) You gave him the slip all right! Come on, Penguins.

All the Penguins dash out of the cage and Flibberty locks the door—throwing the key away as they dash for the bus. Hearing them coming, the Conductor welcomes them aboard

Conductor All aboard, all aboard! (*He changes hats*) First stop the Concert Hall, first stop the Concert Hall.

Krafty Kingfisher, still stunned, gets up to find himself locked in the cage. He rattles the cage as the bus disappears

The bus, with its occupants the Penguins and Flibberty, exits

Kingfisher Aaah, you'll all suffer for this. (*To the audience*) Especially you!

The Policeman enters on his scooter, blowing his whistle and searching for Krafty Kingfisher

Policeman Krafty, Krafty, where are you? Where are you?

The audience tell the Policeman that Krafty Kingfisher is in the cage. The Policeman looks

Well, well. (*He looks delighted*) Behind bars again already, eh?

Kingfisher (*pointing to the audience*) They tricked me. The rotten lot.

Policeman I'm very pleased to hear it. You deserve to be locked up until you learn to behave better.

The Zookeeper enters

Zookeeper I'm sure I had that key a moment ago. (*Seeing the Policeman*) Hallo, Officer; what luck! I wish to report a lost key. Have you found one?
Policeman A lost key? No.

The audience should shout out and point to where Flibberty threw the key. If they do not, the Policeman notices it and points it out to the Zookeeper

Zookeeper (*seeing the key*) Oh. Thank you. (*Going to the cage*) I wouldn't have wanted my little penguin to escape. I . . . (*Seeing Kingfisher inside*) What are *you* doing in there?
Kingfisher (*pointing to the audience*) They tricked me!
Zookeeper But where are the penguins?
Policeman I wouldn't be surprised to hear they've escaped.
Kingfisher Quite right.
Zookeeper What? This is a disaster. You must find them, Officer. What am I . . . Wait a minute. (*To the Policeman*) What is he? (*He points to Krafty Kingfisher*)
Policeman He's Krafty Kingfisher.
Kingfisher Very crafty.
Zookeeper But—how wonderful! Krafty Kingfisher. There's only one of him, and there are thousands of penguins. I'll keep him instead.
Policeman So you don't want me to search for the penguins?
Zookeeper No. They can stay free. Who wants to see penguins when they can see Krafty Kingfisher? (*He changes the notice outside the cage to KRAFTY KINGFISHER*)
Kingfisher Grrrrrrh.
Policeman Splendid. Well, I must away to the Concert. I'm playing my whistle there, you know.

The Policeman scoots off

Zookeeper Bye, bye. Now, Krafty—a little supper? (*He points to the bucket in the cage*)
Kingfisher Grrrrrrh.
Zookeeper Fish? You like fish, don't you?
Kingfisher Wouldn't say I didn't.
Zookeeper Well, there you are then—a whole bucketfull all to yourself.
Kingfisher (*unable to resist the thought of food*) All right. (*He tucks in greedily*)

SONG: ROLL UP! ROLL UP! (Reprise)

Zookeeper (*singing to Krafty Kingfisher*)

I'll feed you well
On fish and such
'Cos I can tell
You like it so much

> I'll keep you spry
> And in good shape;
> Though you may try
> You'll never escape.

Krafty Kingfisher growls angrily, but carries on eating

> Roll up! Roll up!
> For a treat that's cheap
> See my Krafty
> A penny a peep
> Folk will flock from far and near
> They will clap and they will cheer
> When they see this singular
>   Kingfisher Krafty here.

SCENE 6

The Concert Hall

The Concert is about to start. Master Ministrone enters with an ancient gramophone. He winds it up and starts to play a record—a scratchy, out-of-tune fanfare

Ministrone (*after a short burst of fanfare*) My lords, ladies, and-a gentlemen, mesdames, messieurs, signor, signora—a-presenting a concert—fantastic-issimo and bellissimo—to-a celebrate the arrival of spring. (*He puts the record on again for another fanfare burst*) With the Colossal Concert Choir—(*indicating the audience*)—and a-featuring the harmonious singing duo—Mr and Mrs Silly Cuckoo—(*Another fanfare*)

Mr and Mrs Silly Cuckoo enter, giggling and embarrassed, and bow to the audience, who are encouraged to clap by Master Ministrone

—and a-starring the a-one and only, incredibilissimo, sensationalissimo conducter—*Mr Maestro!* (*He puts on the record, causing another ghastly running-down fanfare*)

Mr Maestro enters in the grand manner—carrying the toothbrush as a baton. He acknowledges the welcome of the crowd like a bullfighter

Master Ministrone and the Silly Cuckoos encourage the audience to clap. Mr Maestro ascends the rostrum and taps with the toothbrush

Just as Mr Maestro raises the toothbrush to start, the bus enters with its occupants, the Bus Driver loudly sounding the bell

Mr Maestro looks furious

Maestro (*singing*) Oh. Good gracioso.

Bus Driver (*parking the bus*) Sorry we're late. (*Realizing, he sings*) Sorry we're late.

Flibberty We found Percival's mother and father!

The three Penguins get off the bus followed by the Bus Driver, who changes hats on the way

Maestro (*singing*) Bravo, bravo. Now-a please get-a ready to sing.

The Conductor, Penguins and Flibberty stand with the Silly Cuckoos and Master Ministrone

Conductor Sorry, Mr Maestro. (*He whispers to the Cuckoos*) What are we singing?

Mr Silly Cuckoo The First Day of Springywingy!

Mrs Silly Cuckoo You sillywillybilly.

Ministrone Shhhh!

Mr Maestro taps again with the toothbrush, raises it and, in the quiet, raises it again dramatically

The Policeman enters on his scooter, furiously blowing his whistle

Maestro (*furiously*) Aaah. I don't-a believe it!

Policeman (*parking*) So sorry I'm late. (*Realizing, he sings*) Sorry, Mr Maestro. (*Speaking to the others*) We've caught Krafty Kingfisher at last.

All cheer

Maestro (*singing*) Quiet. Pianissimo, *please*. Now—everybody (*taking in the audience*) please-a sing!

Policeman (*to the Conductor, whispering*) What are we singing?

Conductor The First Day of Spring, of course.

Policeman I don't know the words of that one.

Ministrone Shhh!

Policeman But I don't know the words! How can I sing if I don't know the words? (*To the Audience*) Do you? I bet you don't. Do you? There you are!

Ministrone All-a right!

Master Ministrone rushes off

Mr Maestro starts conducting. The introduction music continues as Master Ministrone brings on the words of the song. Mr Maestro conducts everyone in, and all except the Penguins sing—Mr Maestro encouraging the audience to join in

SONG: THE FIRST DAY OF SPRING

All (*singing*)   It's the first day of spring
                                       It's the first day of spring

                    The worst days of winter
                    Are past
                    The birds are singing
                    The bells are ringing
                    And the newly-born lambs go Baaaah!

Maestro (*after one chorus*)   Encore, encore. And-a much louder.
All (*singing*)   It's the first day of spring
                    It's the first day of spring
                    The worst days of winter
                    Are gone
                    The flowers are growing
                    The breeze is blowing
                    And the first cuckoos sing their song

Maestro (*singing*) Bravissimo, bravo. Now, Master Ministrone—arrange the noises.

Ministrone (*singing*) Yes, Mr Maestro. (*To the audience*) Now, everyone. We want this time to not-a only sing-a the song, but to make-a noises too. I show you—in-a the song we sing about-a the bird singing, so let's-a all *whistle* like birds. Policeman, you help us with your-a whistle.

All practise bird noises

Bravo! Then we sing about-a the bells-a ringing. So let's make "ding dong" noises like-a the bells. Bus Conductor—you can ring-a the bus bell to help us.

All practise bell noises

Very good. What about the lambs? They go baaa-aa-aa! Can-a we all do that—it's-a bit like-a the bus's horn. Percival, can you press the horn for us?

The Penguin goes to the Driver's cab

Let's-a all do lamb noises.

All practise lamb noises

Bravo! What else? Ah! The flowers have to grow. That doesn't need a noise, but we could all a-stand up and be flowers-a growing, yes? Mother Penguin, Father Penguin—can you help us do that?

All practise being flowers growing, led by Mother and Father Penguin miming

And-a finally we have the breeze a-blowing—so we must a-make windy noises. Flibberty, can you do it? Everyone join in with Flibberty.

All practise breeze noises

Bravo! Very good. Now, let's all go through everything—first the birds.

All do bird noises with the Policeman

Let the bells.

All do the noises with the Conductor

The lambs.

All do the noises with the Penguins

The flowers.

All do the movement with Mr and Mrs Penguin

The breezes.

All do the noises with Flibberty

Bravo. Now. Let's-a all sing the song and put in the noises. (*Singing*)
Ready, Mr Maestro.

Maestro (*singing*) Bravo! Take a deep-a breath.

All take a deep breath

Clear your throats.

All clear throats

And-a here we go.

The Zookeeper enters with Krafty Kingfisher on a lead

Zookeeper Can we come in?

Maestro Aaah!

All react to Krafty Kingfisher, especially the Penguin

Zookeeper It's all right—he's on a lead! And he's very happy at the Zoo.

Flibberty Why?

Kingfisher I can have as much fish as I like there! Jubbyjubbyjub!

Maestro (*singing*) Please-a don't interrupt the concert!

Zookeeper But we had to! It's so exciting—at the Zoo the first new lamb
has just been born . . .

*If possible, a live lamb brought on stage would be very popular with the audience
—but clearly this is not always, if ever, practicable!*

Policeman Aaah! How lovely.

Conductor The first lamb of spring.

Maestro (*singing*) What?

Ministrone (*singing*) The first lamb of spring has been born.

Flibberty Then that means . . .

Silly Cuckoos (*together*) The first day of springywingy is here!

Ministrone It's time for your-a cuckoos! Let's-a all sing the song, with the
noises, and ending with Mr and Mrs Silly Cuckoo—the first cuckoos of
spring!

Maestro (*singing*) All-a together!

*All sing the song, with the noises, and ending with the Silly Cuckoos singing
their "cuckoos" perfectly*

Flibberty Spring is here at last!

The music continues as we see a transformation in the set—the lighting changes to warm spring colours, as flowers blossom, trees spring leaves, buds open, etc. All the characters watch in wonder. When the transformation is complete and the music stops, all the characters clap and cheer

Maestro (*singing*) Bravo, bravo!
Ministrone Three cheers for-a spring! Hip hip—
All Hooray!
Ministrone Hip hip—
All Hooray!
Ministrone Hip hip—
All Hooray!

During this the Penguins, especially Percival, look a bit hot and bothered

Flibberty (*noticing*) Percival, what's the matter?

The Penguin mimes that he is too hot

What? What's the matter with him?

The audience is encouraged to tell Flibberty

Of course, it's too hot for penguins in springtime! I told you we had to find your mother and father before spring, or you'd be roasted! And we have! It's time for you—all three of you—to go home.
Policeman Where is their home, Flibberty?
Flibberty Iceland.
Policeman Well, that's a very long way.
Conductor I could take them—in my bus.
Flibberty Would you really?
Conductor Of course—a pleasure.

The Penguins look pleased

Jump aboard and I'll tell the driver.
Flibberty It's a long way for him to drive.
Conductor He won't mind. (*Calling as he gets on the bus*) Driver! (*He changes hats*) Yes, Conductor? (*He changes hats*) First stop, Iceland. (*He changes hats*) Rightyho!
Flibberty Bye, bye, Percival!

The Penguin embraces Flibberty, and mimes "I thank you"

Don't thank me! It's been very exciting.

The Bus Driver changes hats and rings the bell

Silly Cuckoos Goodybye, bye. Goodybye, bye!

All wave and call "good-bye" as the Conductor changes hats, sits in the driver's seat and prepares to drive off

SONG: GOOD-BYE, PENGUINS

All   Good-bye, Penguins
                                 Off you go
                                 Back to the land of ice and snow
                                 Good-bye, Penguins
                                 It's been fun
                                 Glad all you wanted to do is done

Bus Driver   Come for a ride
                                 In my beautiful bus
                                 Travel in comfort
                                 No trouble, no fuss
                                 Come for a treat!
                                 Come take a seat
                                 All aboard
                                 My beautiful bus!

All   Good-bye, Penguins
                                 Good luck, too—

The bus starts off

                                 Thank you for coming, and come back soon
                                 Good-bye, Penguins
                                 (*To the audience*) And to you
                                 Thank you for coming, and come back soon.

                                 CURTAIN

FURNITURE AND PROPERTY LIST

forest backing

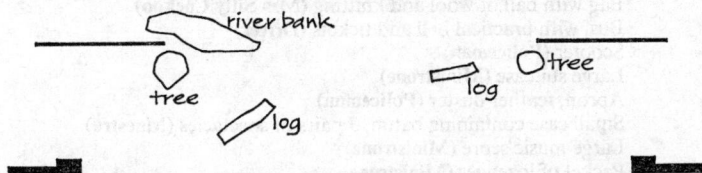
river bank
tree
log
tree
log

ACT I

On stage: 2 trees, several acorns concealed in one
        Logs and river bank

In First Black-Out
Set: Trees and logs to suggest another part of the forest

forest backing (different from scene 1)

tree
log
log

In Second Black-Out
Strike: Trees and logs
Set: Small mound
         Bus stop sign

countryside backing

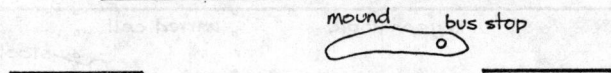
mound
bus stop

In Third Black-Out
Strike: Mound and bus stop
Set: Street scene with wall poster
         Lamp
         Bus stop

Off stage: Suitcase containing framed penguins photo, toothbrush, bar of soap
            (Penguin)
            Fishing rod, wicker basket **(Kingfisher)**
            Old boot, bicycle tyre, tin can, fish (for attachment to **Kingfisher's** rod)
            Shopping bag **(Mr Silly Cuckoo)**
            Bag with ball of wool and knitting **(Mrs Silly Cuckoo)**
            Bus, with practical bell and tickets **(Driver)**
            Scooter **(Policeman)**
            Large suitcase **(Ministrone)**
            Apron, feather duster **(Policeman)**
            Small case containing baton, 3 pairs of spectacles **(Maestro)**
            Large music score **(Ministrone)**
            Packet of lozenges **(Ministrone)**

Personal: **Bus Driver:** second hat (as Conductor)
            Mr Silly Cuckoo: coins
            Policeman: whistle, watch, spectacles

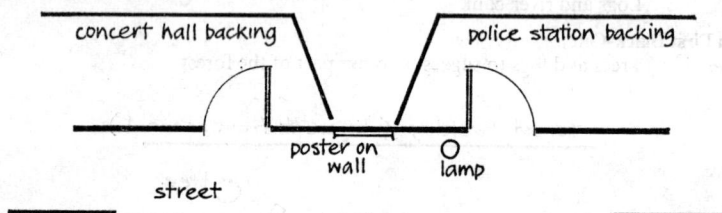

ACT II

On stage: Street scene as end of Act I

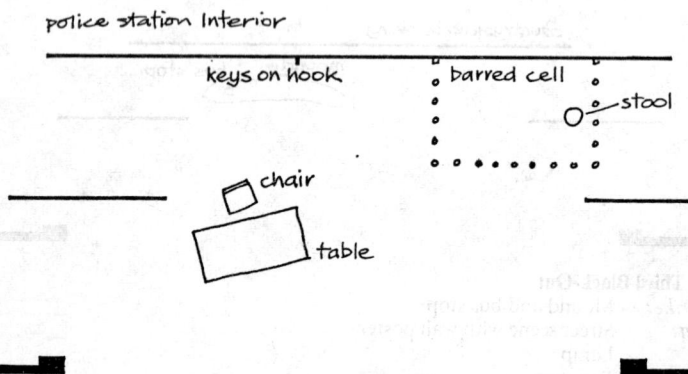

In First Black-Out

Strike: Street scene
Set: Table. *On it:* radio, earphones
Chair
Hook on wall with bunch of keys
Stool in cell

zoo backing with cages

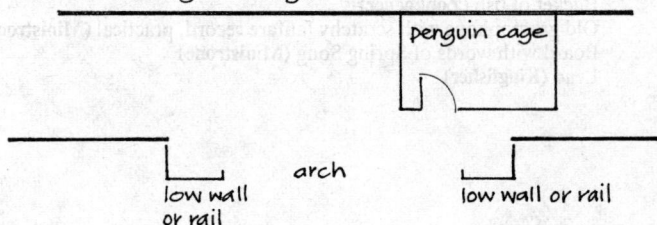

penguin cage

arch

low wall
or rail

low wall or rail

In Second Black-Out

Strike: Police station furniture
Set: Zoo archway with "CLOSED" notice and bell
Cut-out cages
Practical cage marked "PENGUINS". *In it:* stool or log: "KRAFTY
KINGFISHER" notice concealed for Scene 5

In Third Black-Out

Set: Tabs closed over Zoo scene
Small rostrum. *On it:* ornate music stand

tabs - closed in front of Zoo set

music stand
set on rostrum

Scene 6, Zoo set is replaced behind tabs by spring
countryside, which is revealed during the transformation.

In Fourth Black-Out

Strike: Rostrum and stand
Set: Tabs open to reveal Zoo set

In Fifth Black-Out
Set: Tabs closed over Zoo scene
            Rostrum and stand
            Small table for gramophone

During Scene 5
Strike: Zoo set behind tabs
Set: Spring countryside behind tabs for Transformation
Off stage: Large key **(Zookeeper)**
            Bucket of fish **(Zookeeper)**
            Old gramophone with scratchy fanfare record, practical **(Ministrone)**
            Board with words of Spring Song **(Ministrone)**
            Lead **(Kingfisher)**

LIGHTING PLOT

The following is a skeleton plot: individual spots for songs, etc. may be added at the producer's discretion

Property fittings required: nil
Various interior and exterior settings

ACT I

To open:	General effect of winter exterior light	
Cue 1	**Kingfisher** exits *Fade to Black-Out*	(Page 13)
Cue 2	When scene is set *Fade up to similar lighting*	(Page 13)
Cue 3	**Kingfisher** exits *Fade to Black-Out*	(Page 17)
Cue 4	When scene is set *Fade up to similar lighting*	(Page 17)
Cue 5	**Kingfisher** exits *Fade to Black-Out*	(Page 24)
Cue 6	When scene is set *Fade up to street lighting*	(Page 24)

ACT II

To open:	As close of Act I	
Cue 7	Zoo song ends *Fade to Black-Out*	(Page 43)
Cue 8	When scene is set *Fade up to interior lighting, police station*	(Page 43)
Cue 9	**Policeman** exits *Fade to Black-Out*	(Page 45)
Cue 10	When scene is set *Fade up to exterior lighting*	(Page 45)
Cue 11	**Zookeeper** exits *Fade to Black-Out*	(Page 48)
Cue 12	When scene is set *Fade up to Concert Hall lighting*	(Page 48)
Cue 13	**Ministrone:** " . . . we go to the concert." *Fade to Black-Out*	(Page 49)
Cue 14	**Zookeeper:** "I'll feed him well" *Fade up to exterior lighting*	(Page 50)
Cue 15	At end of Zookeeper's song *Fade to Black-Out*	(Page 57)
Cue 16	When scene is set *Fade up to Concert Hall lighting*	(Page 57)
Cue 17	**Flibberty:** "Spring is here at last!" *Lighting change to warm spring colours*	(Page 61)

EFFECTS PLOT

ACT I
SCENE 1

Cue 1 As CURTAIN rises   (Page 1)
      Music: continue until dialogue starts

Cue 2 **Flibberty:** "Come on."   (Page 10)
      Music for mime

SCENE 2
No cues

SCENE 3
No cues

SCENE 4
No cues

SCENE 4
No cues

ACT II
SCENE 1
No cues

SCENE 2

Cue 3 **Policeman** switches on radio   (Page 44)
      Loud trad jazz music

Cue 4 **Policeman** turns off radio   (Page 44)
      Music off

SCENE 3
No cues

SCENE 4
No cues

SCENE 5
No cues

SCENE 5
No cues

SCENE 6
No cues